# DELIVERANCE FROM
# PROPHETIC
# WITCHCRAFT

## Destiny Image Books by Jennifer LeClaire

# DELIVERANCE FROM
# PROPHETIC WITCHCRAFT

## PUT AN END TO THE LINGERING TOXIC EFFECTS OF SATAN'S COUNTERFEIT MESSENGERS

# JENNIFER LECLAIRE

DESTINY IMAGE® PUBLISHERS, INC.

P.O. Box 310, Shippensburg, PA 17257-0310

*"Publishing cutting-edge prophetic resources to supernaturally empower the body of Christ"*

This book and all other Destiny Image and Destiny Image Fiction books are available at Christian bookstores and distributors worldwide.

For more information on foreign distributors, call 717-532-3040.

Reach us on the Internet: www.destinyimage.com.

ISBN 13 TP: 978-0-7684-7282-0

ISBN 13 eBook: 978-0-7684-7283-7

ISBN 13 HC: 978-0-7684-7285-1

ISBN 13 LP: 978-0-7684-7284-4

For Worldwide Distribution, Printed in the USA

1 2 3 4 5 6 7 8 / 27 26 25 24 23

# CONTENTS

# INTRODUCTION

It was a packed house at the Global Prophetic Center's Elijah Company intensive. The people were hungry and expecting to be trained in high-level prophetic ministry. The worship was explosive and the atmosphere ripe for deliverance.

That's when I got a troubling word of knowledge. It wasn't difficult to release, but it was difficult for people to respond publicly due to the associated shame. The word of knowledge spoke of people who aligned with toxic prophets, churches, and ministries despite the Holy Spirit's warning and, as a result, got caught up in prophetic witchcraft.

I sat and waited for people to come up. I knew there were at least a handful in the intensive to whom this word of knowledge applied. I waited and waited. After a few minutes, one by one, five people came up and confessed their experience. Some of the stories were mild. Others were tragic and shared through tears. We broke false covenants and some even received massive deliverance on the spot.

Thank God, there is deliverance from prophetic witchcraft. And that's the message I hope to send loud and clear in the last of this series of books. I can speak firsthand about it because God delivered me from a church where the leader was so hurt and wounded that he gave in to the very spirits he warned against. Little by little, that church got more controlling, less loving, and eventually flat out toxic. I tell parts of my story throughout this book. I hope it will help you understand that anyone can fall into this trap—and anyone can escape.

God wants to deliver you from prophetic witchcraft, even if you willfully ignored the Holy Spirit's warnings. It's the mercy of God, and David understood this well. He wrote, "The righteous cry out, and the Lord hears, and delivers them out of all their troubles" (Ps. 34:17). If you are reading this book, it's likely prophetic witchcraft is one of your troubles—whether it came through a personal relationship, a church, or a network.

Please understand that prophetic witchcraft is nothing new and we won't rid the church of it completely until near the coming of the Lord. Jesus is coming back for a glorious church without spot or wrinkle or any other blemish, including prophetic witchcraft (see Eph. 5:27). Jesus is coming back for a holy church without fault. Part of the purpose of the true five-fold ministry, including prophets, is to prepare the Bride for the Bridegroom (see Eph. 4:11). And we need to get about our Father's business.

In the third and final book of this series, which began with *Discerning Prophetic Witchcraft* and was followed by *Exposing Prophetic Witchcraft*, we'll take a huge leap into freedom. When you see what prophetic witchcraft has done to your soul, a divine indignation will rise up within you, and you will hunger and thirst after righteousness. You'll be equipped to break through false prophetic soul ties, financial and relational witchcraft, sickness, and demons. But more than that, I'll help you fill the void and rebuild trust in the prophetic again—because you need to.

We cannot throw all prophetic ministry out the window because prophetic witchcraft has seeped into some camps. Like I've been saying throughout this trilogy of books, prophetic witchcraft has been around since the Garden of Eden. Yet I believe in prophetic ministry with every fiber of my being. My heart is not to police the prophetic, but to protect the sheep who can hear the voice of God for themselves—and know His heart.

My prayer is that you will find complete freedom from prophetic witchcraft and all its lingering residue, then warn others. My prayer is you will avoid the temptation to go on witch hunts like heresy hunters and throw mud on the entire prophetic movement. My prayer is that you will become a person who has the wisdom to deliver others from prophetic witchcraft while still loving the true voice of God and respecting the true prophets of today. Amen.

# CHAPTER 1

# WHY WE FALL FOR

# PROPHETIC

# WITCHCRAFT

There was once a young prophet who was on fire for God—and he was especially gifted. God raised him up seemingly out of nowhere and he stood before kings. This young prophet delivered difficult words with great confidence and boldness. Even though influential people didn't like his prophetic words, he stood undaunted in the face of persecution. The threats rolled off his back and he kept right on prophesying. He also walked in miraculous healing power—and he couldn't be bought.

Once after this young prophet healed a rebellious influencer, he got an invitation to sit at the power broker's table for dinner. But the young prophet's response was a booming: "Not on your life!

You couldn't pay me enough to get me to sit down with you at a meal in this place. I'm here under God's orders, and he commanded, 'Don't eat a crumb, don't drink a drop, and don't go back the way you came'" (1 Kings 13:8-10 MSG).

This young prophet had integrity. He had discernment. He had the word of the Lord in his mouth. He refused to compromise for power or money or anything else. Despite all this, he was soon deceived by prophetic witchcraft in what is, to me, one of the most troubling accounts in the Bible. It's a literal manifestation of Peter's words about the enemy roaming about like a lion seeking someone to devour (see 1 Pet. 5:8). Let me tell you the rest of the story.

See, there was an old prophet who lived in Bethel. When he heard about his younger counterpart's exploits with the king, he naturally wanted to meet him. When the elder prophet found the man of God, he offered an invitation much the same as the one from the king, which he had emphatically turned down just minutes earlier. The first time the old prophet made the invitation, he essentially got the same answer the king got: "No."

But then something happened. The elder prophet released prophetic witchcraft at the young man: "He said, 'I am also a prophet, just like you. And an angel came to me with a message from God: "Bring him home with you, and give him a good meal!"' But the man was lying. So the holy man went home with him and they had a meal together" (1 Kings 13:18-19 MSG). The young prophet felt pretty good about his decision—until he realized he'd been hit with prophetic witchcraft. We see the deadly account in 1 Kings 13:20-25 (MSG):

> *There they were, sitting at the table together, when the word of God came to the prophet who had brought*

*him back. He confronted the holy man who had come from Judah: "God's word to you: 'You disobeyed God's command; you didn't keep the strict orders your God gave you; you came back and sat down to a good meal in the very place God told you, "Don't eat a crumb; don't drink a drop." For that you're going to die far from home and not be buried in your ancestral tomb."'*

*When the meal was over, the prophet who had brought him back saddled his donkey for him. Down the road a way, a lion met him and killed him. His corpse lay crumpled on the road, the lion on one side and the donkey on the other. Some passersby saw the corpse in a heap on the road, with the lion standing guard beside it.*

Think about it for a minute. If a prophet can be deceived by prophetic witchcraft, who is immune? This young prophet was moving powerfully in his ministry and sought to obey the Lord with all his heart. He turned down the king's offer, but this old prophet with his made-up story about an angel and his false prophetic words led the young man to the grave. Prophetic witchcraft can be deadly. It's doubtful you'll literally get eaten by a lion, but make no mistake— the enemy still comes to steal, kill, and destroy (see John 10:10).

## WHAT IS PROPHETIC WITCHCRAFT?

My first book on this topic, *Discerning Prophetic Witchcraft*, went in-depth into discerning this demonic practice. In case you haven't read that book (and you should) it's helpful to understand what prophetic witchcraft and false prophets are before moving ahead. My second book, *Exposing Prophetic Witchcraft*, offered more particular insights into these unseemly prophetic operations. But it's important to again review what a false prophet is and what prophetic witchcraft is. You don't have to be a false prophet to release prophetic witchcraft.

A false prophet is not one who misses it or one who makes poor judgment calls in ministry operations as they learn and grow. No, a false prophet, in the simplest terms, is one who sets out to deceive. The motive is to gain something to consume upon their own lusts outside the will of God—whether that's money, fame, or some other reward. False prophets don't seek God for what they need, but rather they manipulate their way into what they want.

Maybe you have never heard false prophetic utterance firsthand or witnessed the operation of a false seer—or maybe you were exposed to it but haven't actually discerned these false functions yet. Let me assure you, as one who has walked on the front lines of the prophetic movement for decades, false prophets and false seers are emerging rapidly with manipulative cunning. False prophets appear to the undiscerning eye to be genuine, but they are seeking to devour. They seem sincere, but they are sincerely wrong in motive. It's important to exercise discernment, to examine the fruit rather than being enamored with a spiritual gift, charisma, or a large following.

But false prophets aren't the only ones who operate in prophetic witchcraft. Prophetic witchcraft is false prophecy, but it's the source of the false prophecy that is concerning. While prophecy speaks the mind, will, and heart of God for a person, situation, or nation, prophetic witchcraft can oppose the will of God—or at least lead you into a different direction or out of God's timing. Prophetic witchcraft taps into a spirit other than the Holy Spirit, who is the spirit of prophecy. Since the spirit of prophecy is the testimony of Jesus (see Rev. 19:10), prophetic witchcraft can't be the testimony of Jesus—or what Jesus is saying.

As the head of the church and our Savior, we want to hear the Holy Spirit report what Jesus is saying. Prophetic witchcraft can be what the prophet (or prophetic person) is saying as a means to flatter, manipulate, or control you into giving your time, money, or loyalty to the prophesier. Prophetic witchcraft can also come from a spirit of divination, essentially becoming a message straight from the enemy's camp. The message may sound like something God would say, but that doesn't mean God said it.

What's so tricky for many people is prophetic witchcraft can be true—false prophetic people can speak accurate words—but, again, that doesn't mean the information comes from God. Familiar spirits and other demons set out to deceive, and sometimes they set bait for hungry believers that carries an ounce of truth before selling them a pound of lies. Remember the girl from Thyatira who followed Paul and Silas around proclaiming they were men of God proclaiming the way to salvation? The Acts 16 incident is recorded so we would know that a demon spirit can operate through a person to share truth.

Have you ever wondered why so many believers walk right into prophetic witchcraft traps? Why do we fall for prophetic witchcraft? What causes us to believe false prophecy? Why do we allow ourselves to be manipulated into giving money we don't have for a breakthrough we never get—over and over again? Before we can dive into deliverance from prophetic witchcraft, we first need to understand how and why we open the door to it so once we get delivered we won't open the door again. If we can't discern it and expose it, we can't find lasting deliverance from it. We'll keep falling for it. But, as I always say, an enemy exposed is an enemy defeated.

## THE DESIRE TO GET RICH QUICK

Winning the lottery is a dream come true for many people. Even though the odds are about one in 175 million, many people gamble away their money on this pipe dream. New Yorkers alone spend more than $9 billion a year on lottery tickets. Despite some big wins—sometimes as high as hundreds of millions of dollars—lottery money seems easy come, easy go.

Studies show many stop working or go spend-crazy or give too much away. Study after study reports lottery winners are more likely to go bankrupt within three to five years than the average American. Most believers don't play the lottery, but they do sow into false prophets in hopes of getting that Deuteronomy 1:11 return. That verse, which is commonly used among false prophets, reads: "May the Lord God of your fathers make you a thousand times more numerous than you are, and bless you as He has promised you!" Those are better odds than most trifectas at the horse races!

The desire to get rich quick almost always leads to disaster. The Bible warns us over and over again of this reality. First Timothy 6:10 makes it clear: "For the love of money is a root of all kinds of evil, for which some have strayed from the faith in their greediness, and pierced themselves through with many sorrows." If you have the love of money in your heart, you have common ground with the false prophet who's working to deceive you. Since you're already deceived by making money an idol, you're an easy take.

Proverbs 28:20 warns, "A faithful man will abound with blessings, but he who hastens to be rich will not go unpunished." And Hebrews 13:5 warns, "Let your conduct be without covetousness; be content with such things as you have." First Timothy 6:9 admonishes, "But those who desire to be rich fall into temptation and a snare, and into many foolish and harmful lusts which drown men in destruction and perdition." And let's not forget 1 John 2:15-17:

> *Do not love the world or the things in the world. If anyone loves the world, the love of the Father is not in him. For all that is in the world—the lust of the flesh, the lust of the eyes, and the pride of life—is not of the Father but is of the world. And the world is passing away, and the lust of it; but he who does the will of God abides forever.*

God gives you the power to create wealth, and He desires that you be in health and prosper even as your soul prospers (see 3 John 1:2). But we have to do things His way. There are no shortcuts to prosperity. Deuteronomy 28 offers a list of blessings for the obedient. One of them is, "The Lord will command the blessing on you in your storehouses and in all to which you set your hand, and He will bless you in the land which the Lord your God is giving you" (Deut. 28:8). When we obey Him, we don't need to depend on get rich quick schemes. Get rich quick schemes are not the way of God and typically put us in bondage.

## DESPERATE FOR BREAKTHROUGH

Desperation is not always a bad thing, but desperation can cause you to make bad decisions if you leave Jesus out of the equation. Yes, there are times when we find ourselves in desperate financial situations. I know because I've been there. When I first moved out of my parents' home at eighteen years old, I was largely penniless. I had a hard time surviving on my own. I whittled down to ninety-five pounds, and I'm over five-foot-seven.

Thank God, I never did anything stupid in that desperation, but many people do. People sell their bodies out of desperation for money. People shoplift out of desperation for money. People pawn family heirlooms out of desperation for money. Desperation can lead you into danger—including the danger of prophetic witchcraft.

Real prophets can give you strategy for breakthrough in difficult times. Elisha prophesied to a widow whose sons were about to be taken away because she could not pay her debt. The woman was beyond desperate. Elisha asked her what she had in her house—not so he could take it in exchange for a breakthrough but so he could show her how God will use what's in your hand. Second Kings 4:3-7 tells the rest:

> *Then he said, "Go, borrow vessels from everywhere, from all your neighbors—empty vessels; do not gather just a few. And when you have come in, you shall shut the door behind you and your sons; then pour it into all those vessels, and set aside the full ones."*
>
> *So she went from him and shut the door behind her and her sons, who brought the vessels to her; and she poured*

*it out. Now it came to pass, when the vessels were full, that she said to her son, "Bring me another vessel."*

*And he said to her, "There is not another vessel." So the oil ceased. Then she came and told the man of God. And he said, "Go, sell the oil and pay your debt; and you and your sons live on the rest."*

This is an example of a financial breakthrough, but people get desperate in many areas. I've seen sorcerers casting spells over wayward spouses in the name of Jesus—for a fee. I've seen false prophets promising deliverance only if you sow a seed to God that's bigger than what you gave the witches and warlocks. I've seen people sell healing cloths and healing oils that came from Walmart and weren't even prayed over.

Desperation is not bad so long as it's funneled toward the Lord. The woman with the issue of blood was desperate to be healed. Mark 5:26 reveals she, "had suffered many things from many physicians. She had spent all that she had and was no better, but rather grew worse." This woman went to the real prophet, Jesus, and received a breakthrough without sowing a seed. Her faith made her well.

## FLATTERING PROPHECIES

"You look like you've lost twenty pounds." Those were the words of someone who hadn't seen me in a long time. The truth is, I had gained about twenty pounds. That's called flattery, defined as insincere or excessive praise. Proverbs 29:5 says, "A man who flatters his neighbor spreads a net for his feet." Think about it for a minute.

Why do people flatter you? Clearly, people "butter you up" because they want something from you. Psalm 55:21 warns, "The words of his mouth were smoother than butter, but war was in his heart; his words were softer than oil, yet they were drawn swords."

We all know Jezebel flatters her victims—and so do Jezebelic prophets. People operating in this spirit will offer insincere compliments—and if you're insecure you'll fall for it. Usually, false prophets offer spiritual compliments, such as, "Oh, your discernment is so sharp. Your prophecy is so accurate. You really flow well with the Holy Spirit." This is meant to disarm you. If they praise you for being discerning, they figure that perhaps you won't discern them. Remember, people only flatter you when they want something from you—and they often use prophecy to get it.

Paul warned, "For those who are such do not serve our Lord Jesus Christ, but their own belly, and by smooth words and flattering speech deceive the hearts of the simple" (Rom. 16:18). Jude likewise warned, "These are grumblers, complainers, walking according to their own lusts; and they mouth great swelling words, flattering people to gain advantage" (Jude 1:16). Ezekiel warned of flattering divination (see Ezek. 12:24).

Real prophets stay away from flattering words like the plague. Paul wrote:

> *But as we have been approved by God to be entrusted with the gospel, even so we speak, not as pleasing men, but God who tests our hearts. For neither at any time did we use flattering words, as you know, nor a cloak for covetousness—God is witness* (1 Thessalonians 2:4-5).

Flattery is dangerous both for the one who does the flattering and the one who flatters, and God will expose the smooth operators. Solomon offered these wise words:

> *He who hates, disguises it with his lips, and lays up deceit within himself; when he speaks kindly, do not believe him, for there are seven abominations in his heart; though his hatred is covered by deceit, his wickedness will be revealed before the assembly* (Proverbs 26:24-26).

David prayed, "May the Lord cut off all flattering lips" (Ps. 12:3). Indeed, God will answer that prayer.

## WHY PROPHETIC FLATTERY WORKS

Why does prophetic flattery work? Again, flattery, or false praise, taps into someone's insecurities. People who have low self-esteem or are starving for attention will fall for flattery almost every time, even if they have the gift of discernment. An old Italian proverb says, "He that flatters you more than you desire either has deceived you or wishes to deceive."

Sometimes, prophetic flattery works because people have itching ears. Paul wrote:

> *For the time will come when they will not endure sound doctrine, but according to their own desires, because*

*they have itching ears, they will heap up for themselves teachers; and they will turn their ears away from the truth, and be turned aside to fables* (2 Timothy 4:3-4).

This was also a problem in Isaiah's day:

*That this is a rebellious people, lying children, children who will not hear the law of the Lord; who say to the seers, "Do not see," and to the prophets, "Do not prophesy to us right things; speak to us smooth things, prophesy deceits"* (Isaiah 30:9-10).

And God warned through Jeremiah, "Do not believe them, even though they speak smooth words to you" (Jer. 12:6). But often we do believe them. We believe Jezebel's prophets.

Jezebel's prophets, who are among the company of false prophets and a steady source of prophetic witchcraft, prey on people who have hurts and wounds. Jezebel puts hooks in the hurts and woos you through your wounds. I wrote these words in my book *The Spiritual Warrior's Guide to Defeating Jezebel*:

Are you harboring unresolved hurts and wounds, rebellion, unforgiveness, overblown insecurities, hidden fears or rejection? When we knowingly or unknowingly walk in rebellion, we open ourselves up to Jezebel's influence. It is rebellious to choose not to forgive—and our hurts and wounds will never fully heal until we've released those who hurt and wounded us.

Flattery is an effective tool for manipulating you if you have insecurities and hidden fears of rejection. You will want to receive the "kind" words or puffed-up prophecies because you want to believe they are true. Once you take Jezebel's bait, this spirit can manipulate you. Rejection causes many varieties of vulnerabilities. If you walk under the shroud of rejection you probably work overtime to gain approval, and Jezebel with its flattery is often right there to take advantage of you and put you to work for its wicked tasks.

If you have unresolved hurts and wounds, false prophets will work to victimize you.

Speaking of Jesus, Psalm 147:3 says, "He heals the brokenhearted and binds up their wounds." Sometimes deliverance cannot come before inner healing comes. We know, for example, that you must forgive to get delivered. But if deep wounds are present, it's like untangling a knot. People have to confront their pain and the source of their pain, then forgive the one who hurt them. Only then can the healing begin. That process in and of itself brings a measure of freedom and positions you for deliverance from prophetic witchcraft.

So how can you discern the difference between flattery and a sincere compliment? If the compliment makes you feel uncomfortable, it may be flattery. If the person complimenting you is giving the same compliment to everyone else, it's probably flattery. If their praise for you is too frequent and excessive, that's a sure sign of flattery.

## SELFISH AMBITION

One of my spiritual sons got caught up in prophetic witchcraft. I'll always remember when I saw him dressed the exact same way as eight other guys on a false prophet's team at a conference. I knew something was terribly wrong. He only stuck around that prophetic cult for about five months, and when he left he came to me to share the experience.

When I asked him why he fell for it, he humbly acknowledged it was selfish ambition. The false prophet was promising platforms and promotions. The young man was sure if he hitched his star to the false prophet's wagon, his ministry would grow. Instead, he and his wife wasted time and money and lost ministry momentum. Thankfully, God restored all that was lost. If you have selfish ambition, false prophets will locate you, use you, and abuse you.

James 3:14-16 (ESV) makes the dangers of selfish ambition absolutely clear:

> But if you have bitter jealousy and selfish ambition in your hearts, do not boast and be false to the truth. This is not the wisdom that comes down from above, but is earthly, unspiritual, demonic. For where jealousy and selfish ambition exist, there will be disorder and every vile practice.

Read that again. Selfish ambition has poisoned too many in the Body of Christ. Too many want to make their name great at the expense of making Jesus' name great. They want a bigger platform, more power, more influence, and more impact for their sake rather than the sake of the Gospel. This is an age-old problem that even manifested in Christ's disciples over two thousand years ago. Consider Luke 22:24-27:

> *Now there was also a dispute among them, as to which of them should be considered the greatest. And He said to them, "The kings of the Gentiles exercise lordship over them, and those who exercise authority over them are called 'benefactors.' But not so among you; on the contrary, he who is greatest among you, let him be as the younger, and he who governs as he who serves. For who is greater, he who sits at the table, or he who serves? Is it not he who sits at the table? Yet I am among you as the One who serves."*

That was not the first time the disciples argued over who would be the greatest. Back in Luke 9:46 they were also disputing over the issue. Another time, the mother of John and James asked Jesus to let her sons—the sons of thunder—sit at His right and left hand in the coming Kingdom. You can see the selfish ambition and pride in the hearts of James and John:

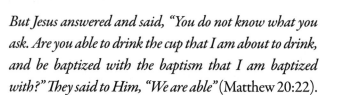

> *But Jesus answered and said, "You do not know what you ask. Are you able to drink the cup that I am about to drink, and be baptized with the baptism that I am baptized with?" They said to Him, "We are able"* (Matthew 20:22).

What arrogance! Thank God, they grew up and saw the light. Not everyone who is ambitious is a false prophet, but unchecked ambition leads nowhere good.

# CHAPTER 2

# WHAT PROPHETIC WITCHCRAFT DOES
# TO YOUR SOUL

I knew I was deceived. I just didn't know if I was deceived by church leaders or the enemy. But in a moment of clarity, I decided it was possible the leaders of the church I had labored in for eight years were the ones in deception. After getting outside counsel, the light came on and I could see the truth that set me free.

Prophetic witchcraft confuses and deceives your soul. Your soul is your mind, will, emotions, imaginations, reasoning, and intellect. Prophetic witchcraft sows subtle seeds of deception in our souls. Prophetic witchcraft renews our mind to lies, bends our will to serve idols, and exploits our emotions for greedy gain. Prophetic witchcraft releases vain imaginations, reprograms your reasoning, and infects your intellect.

You are a spirit, you have a soul, and you live in a body (see 1 Thess. 5:23). When you align with prophetic witchcraft, it does plenty of damage to your soul, and it grieves the Lord. Remember,

Jesus died for your soul. Your soul belongs to God (see Ezek. 18:4). As such, we should be good stewards of our soul.

Put it simply, prophetic witchcraft does damage to your soul. It's difficult to love the Lord with all your heart, soul, and mind when you are living under a cloud of prophetic witchcraft that's driving you into thoughts, feelings, and actions that grieve His heart. God wants us to be in health and prosper even as our soul prospers (see 3 John 1:2). But prophetic witchcraft toxifies our soul.

Prophetic witchcraft releases dullness and death to the soul through the power of words. There is death and life in the power of the tongue (see Prov. 18:21). Thank God, He can restore your soul (see Ps. 23:3). Now consider this: Psalm 19:7 (ESV) tells us, "The law of the Lord is perfect, reviving the soul."

## PROPHETIC WITCHCRAFT RENEWS YOUR MIND TO LIES

Think about it. Faith comes by hearing, and hearing by the Word of God (see Rom. 10:17). Likewise, faith in the false comes through continually hearing the false. Our minds are renewed, in large part, by what we hear, what we say, and what we meditate on. That's why Paul chronicled these Holy Spirit-inspired words in Romans 12:1-2:

> *I beseech you therefore, brethren, by the mercies of God, that you present your bodies a living sacrifice, holy, acceptable to God, which is your reasonable service. And do not be conformed to this world, but be transformed by the renewing of your mind, that you may prove what is that good and acceptable and perfect will of God.*

This is a serious warning. *Beseech* means to urge. Mind renewal was such a strong conviction in Paul's life that he put a demand on the Romans—and us—not to allow the spirit of the world to pollute our souls but to let God's Word revive and renew our souls. Prophetic witchcraft conforms our minds to the ways of the world. John wrote in 1 John 2:15-17 (NLT):

> *Do not love this world nor the things it offers you, for when you love the world, you do not have the love of the Father in you. For the world offers only a craving for physical pleasure, a craving for everything we see, and pride in our achievements and possessions. These are not from the Father, but are from this world. And this world is fading away, along with everything that people crave. But anyone who does what pleases God will live forever.*

The good news is you can reverse the curse of prophetic witchcraft on your mind. God wants to break in with light and deliver you from the ties and the lies that bind. He can accelerate the renewal of your mind by deploying truth bombs to blow up every evil seed the enemy sowed in your soul.

## PROPHETIC WITCHCRAFT BUILDS ENEMY STRONGHOLDS

Little by little, prophetic witchcraft builds strongholds in the mind. Biblically, a stronghold is like a castle in the mind—a fortress, an argument, demonic reasonings, and wisdom. James speaks of a wisdom that does not descend from heaven and calls it "earthly, sensual, demonic" (James 3:15). Thankfully, the weapons of our warfare are not carnal but mighty to destroy strongholds in our minds (see 2 Cor. 10:4).

## PROPHETIC WITCHCRAFT LEADS YOU INTO CARNALITY

Paul asked the church at Galatia, "O foolish Galatians! Who has bewitched you that you should not obey the truth, before whose eyes Jesus Christ was clearly portrayed among you as crucified?" (Gal. 3:1). Prophetic witchcraft takes your mind off Christ and sets it on the things of the flesh. It manipulates your soul and distracts your heart from the main thing.

Prophetic witchcraft taps into your carnal nature and fleshly desires, which can be idolatry. This is dangerous long term. Paul told us in Romans 8:5-6, "For those who live according to the flesh set their minds on the things of the flesh, but those who live according to the Spirit, the things of the Spirit. For to be carnally minded is death, but to be spiritually minded is life and peace." The good news is you can reverse the curse and start sowing to the Spirit again.

## PROPHETIC WITCHCRAFT MAKES YOU DULL

Prophetic witchcraft makes it more difficult to hear God's voice. When we don't make a habit of pressing into God's presence for ourselves and waiting for His still small voice to speak to us directly, we are prime targets for prophetic witchcraft. When we look to people over God for direction, we are on a pathway to dependence on false voices.

The writer of Hebrews spoke of those who became "dull of hearing" (see Heb. 5:11). Think about it. Jesus spoke of those whose hearts had grown so callous they could hardly hear with their ears and their eyes were closed (see Matt. 13:15). Dull in the context of these Scriptures means slow, sluggish, indolent, languid and, yes, dull, according to *The KJV New Testament Greek Lexicon*. *Merriam-Webster*'s dictionary defines *dull* as "slow in perception or sensibility."

Prophetic witchcraft releases words that often defy the Word of God—or the timing of God—for your life. If you give your ear to it, you will be slow to hear instead of quick to listen to the truth. Think about it for a minute. When a knife is dull it can't even cut through a tomato. When your hearing is dull you may follow the voice of a stranger because you can't tell the difference between the voice of God and the voice of the enemy. You can't accurately cut through the clutter of voices in the spirit.

That's why intimacy with God is so important. Jesus said His sheep follow Him because they know His voice (John 10:4). That Greek word for *know* is *eido*. According to *The KJV New Testament Greek Lexicon*, it means to perceive by any of the senses and to have regard for one, cherish and pay attention. If we don't get to know Jesus—to regard, cherish, and pay attention to His voice—we are in danger of mistaking a stranger's voice for His voice (see John 10:5). The good news is you can draw close to God and He can re-open your eyes and ears. You can be more sensitive than ever to His heart.

## PROPHETIC WITCHCRAFT BENDS YOUR WILL

Prophetic witchcraft bends your will away from God into idolatry and immorality. God has given us a free will. Your will is used to express your desires, choices, actions, consent or disagreement. When Christ walked the earth, fully God and fully man, He had a will but He submitted it completely to God. We need to do the same, but when we submit to prophetic witchcraft we find our will bending toward sinful pursuits.

God will not violate our will, but the enemy does everything he can to bend our free will to his pleasure. Speaking of those who oppose the truth, Paul wrote in 2 Timothy 2:26 (NLT): "Then they will come to their senses and escape from the devil's trap. For they have been held captive by him to do whatever he wants." Prophetic witchcraft releases a darkness in your soul that distorts your will.

When we submit ourselves to God and resist the devil, he will flee from us (see James 4:7). When we don't resist prophetic witchcraft—whether it's due to ignorance, idolatry, or some other illness of the soul—we are not submitted to God. When our will is not submitted to God, the enemy has a legal right to steal, kill, and destroy (see John 10:10). When our will is not submitted to God, prophetic witchcraft devours (see 1 Pet. 5:8). The good news is you can realign your will to God through the gift of repentance.

## PROPHETIC WITCHCRAFT SULLIES YOUR IMAGINATION

Prophetic witchcraft sullies your imagination. Imagination, which is part of the soulish realm, is neither good nor bad. *Merriam-Webster* defines *imagination* as "the act or power of forming a mental image of something not present to the senses or never before wholly perceived in reality" and "a creation of the mind."

Your imagination is a gift from God, and the enemy wants to pervert it. Paul told the church at Corinth that eye has not seen, nor ear heard, nor the heart of man imagined what God has prepared for those who love Him (see 1 Cor. 2:9 ESV). God wants us to imagine ourselves healed, whole, and prosperous because His Word tells us by His stripes we are healed (see 1 Pet. 2:24) and that He wants us to prosper and be in health even as our soul prospers (see 3 John 1:2).

Prophetic witchcraft skews the holy imagination with what the Bible calls vain imaginations. Paul spoke about the vain imagination in Romans 1:21 (KJV) in context of sinners: "Because that, when they knew God, they glorified him not as God, neither were thankful; but became vain in their imaginations, and their foolish heart was darkened." When our imagination becomes vain—which means showing undue or excessive pride, marked by futility, foolish, silly, and having no real value—we are heading for destruction.

Shortly before God told Noah He was going to destroy the earth with a flood and commissioned him to build an ark to preserve a remnant of people and animals, this happened: "The Lord observed the extent of human wickedness on the earth, and he saw that everything they thought or imagined was consistently and totally evil" (Gen. 6:5 NLT). Again, a sullied imagination leads to destruction.

Later, when the people set out to make a name for themselves by building a tower called Babel:

*The Lord said, "Behold, they are one [unified] people, and they all have the same language. This is only the beginning of what they will do [in rebellion against Me], and now no evil thing they imagine they can do will be impossible for them. Come, let Us (Father, Son, Holy Spirit) go down and there confuse and mix up their language, so that they will not understand one another's speech"* (Genesis 11:6-7 AMP).

Your imagination should be yielded to God and sanctified. God doesn't want you imagining vain, foolish, silly things that have no value. He doesn't want you using that creative ability the wrong way. Likewise, He doesn't want you to receive ministry from those whose hearts are devising wicked imaginations (see Prov. 6:18). When the imagination—the thought—doesn't line up with God's thoughts, He wants you to cast those imaginations down before they renew your mind to a false prophetic reality.

Paul put it this way: "Casting down imaginations, and every high thing that exalteth itself against the knowledge of God, and bringing into captivity every thought to the obedience of Christ" (2 Cor. 10:5 KJV). *Kathariereo*, the word for *casting* in the Greek, has a violent connotation. It means "to pull down, demolish; with the use of force: to throw down; to destroy," according to *The KJV New Testament Greek Lexicon*.

This command is imperative. What you don't cast down will take root. What takes root will renew your mind. What renews your mind will inform your words and deeds. What informs your words and deeds will shape your life. The Holy Spirit wants to use your imagination to lead you into His plans and purposes for your life—to show you what's possible. Prophetic witchcraft uses your imagination against you to pervert your mind and heart. Don't let it. The good news is you can consecrate your imagination again and begin to imagine His will.

## PROPHETIC WITCHCRAFT INFECTS YOUR INTELLECT

Prophetic witchcraft infects your intellect. Your intellect is your capacity for knowledge and intelligent thought. God wants us to grow in the knowledge of His heart. He wants us to think on things that are good, lovely, excellent, and praiseworthy so we can tap into His higher thoughts. He wants to transform our lives through mind renewal so we can discern His will rightly and walk in prosperity in all areas of our lives (see Rom. 12:2).

Prophetic witchcraft blinds our mind and warps our intellect (see 2 Cor. 3:14). We stop tapping into God's higher thoughts and tap into witchcraft thoughts—or we don't think for ourselves at all. Instead of iron sharpening iron, your intellect becomes dull. Your critical thinking skills go out the window. You go along with group-think until you no longer know right from wrong. You eventually forfeit intelligent thought.

Prophetic witchcraft corrupts the intellect. Paul warned his spiritual son Titus not to listen to commands of people who have turned away from the truth (see Titus 1:14 NLT). The apostle went on to say, "To the pure all things are pure, but to those who are defiled and unbelieving nothing is pure; but even their mind and conscience are defiled" (Titus 1:15). People operating in prophetic witchcraft are defiled and they want to corrupt your intellect for greedy gain. The good news is you can dedicate your intellect to God and He will purify it.

## PROPHETIC WITCHCRAFT DARKENS YOUR DISCERNMENT

Prophetic witchcraft darkens your discernment. Discernment is "the quality of being able to grasp and comprehend what is obscure," also "an act of perceiving or discerning something," according to *Merriam-Webster*'s dictionary. *Discerning* means "able to see and understand people, things, or situations clearly and intelligently."

Discernment is the ability to distinguish between good and evil. It's the ability to judge a righteous judgment (see John 7:24). Discernment is not suspicion or criticism. But when prophetic witchcraft starts darkening your discernment, that's what you are left with. Ironically, suspicion blocks true discernment. You end up second-guessing yourself and what you see. You may even become paranoid.

## PROPHETIC WITCHCRAFT RUINS YOUR REASONINGS

God has blessed you with the ability to reason. That reasoning helps you dissect and discern situations. It helps you comprehend or infer what is being said or done so you can draw the right conclusion and react accordingly. Reasoning helps you make rational decisions about your time and money and in relationships. Prophetic witchcraft ruins your reasonings.

Paul noted, "When I was a child, I spoke and thought and reasoned as a child. But when I grew up, I put away childish things" (1 Cor. 13:11 NLT). God wants us to reason together with Him (see Isa. 1:18). He wants to be part of our reasoning process. He wants to help us discern what is going on so we can respond instead of react. Prophetic witchcraft ruins your reasoning. Prophetic witchcraft confuses and clouds your reasoning to the point that you make poor decisions. The good news is God can restore your reasoning if you ask Him.

## PROPHETIC WITCHCRAFT RESULTS IN DISAPPOINTMENT

Prophetic witchcraft brings disappointment. Prophetic witchcraft pumps you up with false prophecy that will never come to pass because it never came from God. Prophetic witchcraft offers false hope in promises God didn't make as the bedrock of faith. With that, over time prophetic witchcraft damages one's faith in God even though His Spirit never opened His mouth. Solomon noted that hope deferred makes the heart sick (see Prov. 13:12).

True hope does not disappoint (see Rom. 5:5). When we trust in the voice of the Lord and His timing, we will not be disappointed (see Ps. 22:5). Prophetic witchcraft, by contrast, leaves you defeated when you had high expectations and hope in a false prophecy. Prophetic witchcraft will always fail to meet your expectations. It will frustrate your faith. Prophetic witchcraft brings disappointment, discouragement, discontent, dissatisfaction, and dismay. The good news is God can reappoint you.

## PROPHETIC WITCHCRAFT BRAINWASHES YOU

Prophetic witchcraft ultimately brainwashes you. Brainwashing is "a forcible indoctrination to induce someone to give up basic political, social, or religious beliefs and attitudes to accept contrasting regimented ideas; persuasion by propaganda or salesmanship," according to *Merriam-Webster*'s dictionary. Brainwashing hijacks your beliefs and introduces error. The good news is, God can wash you with the water of His Word and teach you the truth.

## PROPHETIC WITCHCRAFT LEADS TO SHAME

Those who hope in the Lord will never be put to shame (see Ps. 25:3). But prophetic witchcraft often brings shame into the lives of those who bank on it. You feel foolish once you've figured out you were hoodwinked. You feel ashamed of yourself for believing a lie.

In the Garden of Eden, the enemy used prophetic witchcraft against Eve. She believed the false prophecy that if she ate from the Tree of the Knowledge of Good and Evil her eyes would be opened and she would be like God. The deception was she was already like God in that she was made in His image. She knew what she needed to know. When Adam and Eve ate the forbidden fruit, their eyes were indeed opened, but it was a rude awakening. Genesis 3:7-10 reveals the sudden shame that came upon them:

> *Then the eyes of both of them were opened, and they knew that they were naked; and they sewed fig leaves together and made themselves coverings. And they*

*heard the sound of the Lord God walking in the garden in the cool of the day, and Adam and his wife hid themselves from the presence of the Lord God among the trees of the garden. Then the Lord God called to Adam and said to him, "Where are you?" So he said, "I heard Your voice in the garden, and I was afraid because I was naked; and I hid myself."*

The good news is, God can break that shame off your soul. In Isaiah 61:7, God said, "Instead of your shame you shall have double honor, and instead of confusion they shall rejoice in their portion. Therefore in their land they shall possess double; everlasting joy shall be theirs."

## PROPHETIC WITCHCRAFT OPENS YOU TO DEMONIZATION

Prophetic witchcraft opens you up to demonization. When you believe words laced with prophetic witchcraft, you are believing a lie. In a way, you are renewing your mind to darkness. You have come into agreement with dark forces. Even if you did so unknowingly, you turned to a medium. You may even have sought them out for a prophetic word in desperation.

Leviticus 19:31 tells us starkly, "Give no regard to mediums and familiar spirits; do not seek after them, to be defiled by them: I am the Lord your God." God wants to speak to you directly, so when you are hungrier for a word from a prophet than you are for God, the giver of life-giving words, you are defiling yourself. You are setting yourself up for deception and even transference of spirits. I wrote at length about the transference of spirits in my book *Discerning Prophetic Witchcraft*.

## PROPHETIC WITCHCRAFT LEAVES YOU DECEIVED

Prophetic witchcraft leaves you deceived. I've said it many times before. The prophetic word you don't judge is the prophetic word that can derail your life. Prophetic witchcraft is deceptive and those who are deceived and being deceived are the ones propagating it (see 2 Tim. 3:13). God delivered you out of the dark kingdom of deception, but prophetic witchcraft puts you back in a measure of bondage.

Paul said, "Stand fast therefore in the liberty by which Christ has made us free, and do not be entangled again with a yoke of bondage" (Gal. 5:1). Jesus set you free so you would be free indeed, but if you don't walk in the truth you know—if you walk in prophetic lies—you can find yourself in dark deception or even delusion. That's why Paul said, "Watch, stand fast in the faith, be brave, be strong" (1 Cor. 16:13).

Paul was upset with some in the church at Corinth, which was known for operating in spiritual gifts. He wrote, "But I fear, lest somehow, as the serpent deceived Eve by his craftiness, so your minds may be corrupted from the simplicity that is in Christ" (2 Cor. 11:3). He also wrote, "For you put up with fools gladly, since you yourselves are wise! For you put up with it if one brings you into bondage, if one devours you, if one takes from you, if one exalts himself, if one strikes you on the face" (2 Cor. 11:19-20).

Prophetic witchcraft has been an issue from the beginning. And so has deception. The good news is you can ask the Lord to break any deception off your mind and you will begin to see clearly again.

## SIGNS YOUR SOUL IS TOXIC

Solomon said pleasant words are like a honeycomb, like sweetness to the soul. Words of prophetic witchcraft, by contrast, can cause bitterness in the soul (see Prov. 16:24). We know words can sink deep into one's heart (see Prov. 18:8). So how can you assess prophetic witchcraft's damage to your soul? Some signs of soul damage are obvious and some are more subtle. Pray as you read through this:

### Serious control issues:

When you've been controlled, you often wind up with control issues—if you are not healed. Some people issue inner vows declaring, "I will never let anyone control me again." This attracts demons into your soul and, many times, you become the very thing you hate. You become a controller. By contrast, some people who have been controlled wind up unable to demonstrate self-control.

### Suffering severe trust issues:

When prophetic witchcraft has held you captive, you may have severe trust issues, mostly with prophets or leaders. You may not want to submit to legitimate spiritual authority because you were hurt by illegitimate spiritual authority. Unfortunately, that may stunt your growth. Everyone needs a trusted leader in their life as there is safety in wise counsel.

### Carrying a victim mentality:

If you have a victim mentality, your soul is damaged. We'll talk more about deliverance from a victim mentality later in the book. With this victim mentality, you may be easily offended or defensive and hypersensitive about being deceived. You may even mock the true work of the Lord because it doesn't fit into your conservative paradigm.

### Dealing in double-mindedness:

Prophetic witchcraft can leave you double-minded, unable to make wise decisions. James 1:8 tells us a double-minded man is unstable in all his ways. Therefore, instability marks your life. You may even question if what you experienced was truly prophetic witchcraft and be tempted to return to the witch's house.

### Walking in fear instead of love:

Fear brings torment. Your mind may be tormented by what the ones who released prophetic witchcraft at you may conjure up against you next. You may fear the slander or the curses. You may fear losing friends. You may fear falling into deception again. Peace is absent and you are physically and emotionally worn out.

### Vanishing with a vagabond spirit:

People who have been attacked by prophetic witchcraft often church hop. Because they've been so hurt and wounded, they hop to another church at the tiniest (and often imaginary) sign something may be wrong. Or they church hop before anyone can get close enough to them to hurt them again. Or they go to multiple churches but won't submit to any leader. They aren't planted any-where so they don't blossom anywhere.

## Oozing resentment, unforgiveness, and bitterness:

You may not see it at first, but out of your wounded heart come words of resentment, unforgiveness, and bitterness. You are angry about what happened to you, and that anger is covering up the pain. You may deny the unforgiveness, but the torment in your soul won't leave until you loose the ones who wronged you.

Of course, there are many other signs of a toxic soul, such as feeling damaged or worthless, struggling with perfectionism or pro-crastination, living with anxiety, depression, or fear or addictions of any kind. When souls are damaged, nightmares may result. You may manifest with various illnesses, including skin issues as your skin literally weeps. You may experience memory loss or flashbacks from the trauma your soul experienced.

When your soul is toxic, you may feel helpless or hopeless, deeply hurt and wounded, pessimistic and protective of your heart. You may wall people out and even wall God out. You may feel discour-aged, like you want to give up. You may walk in disappointment, feel like running away, or even deny anything happened. You may shut out the work of the Holy Spirit because you were duped by a counterfeit anointing. Thankfully, through the pages of this book, the power of the Holy Spirit, and the name of Jesus you can find deliverance from prophetic witchcraft.

CHAPTER 3

# SIGNS YOU'RE IN A
# PROPHETIC CULT

When cults are exposed, they make major news headlines. Some ministries or churches accused of cult status are truly cultish, and others are not. But the flood of "Christian" cult activity should urge you to sharpen your cult identification skills. Most Christian cult followers had no idea what they were getting into until they were already brainwashed adherents to warped religions. Some escaped to tell their stories. Others died in their deception.

ABC's 20/20 exposed the shocking truth about life inside Warren Jeffs' Fundamentalist Latter-Day Saints Church. The cult leader was convicted and jailed for sexual abuse of young girls. He's known for ordering married couples to stop having sex and handpicked fifteen men to father all the church's children. That's clearly a cult. Yet his eight thousand followers continue to believe he's a persecuted prophet.

ABC 7 reported on the Scientology controversy in Washington, DC. L. Ron Hubbard's creation theory highlights a despot named Xenu sending surplus beings to volcanoes on earth. Scientology officials deny cult status, but this is clearly a cult. And Ontario officials investigated allegations of abuse and polygamy under the leadership of a "prophet" named Fred King from the Reorganized Church of Jesus Christ of Latter Day Saints.

Fox also sent undercover reporters to investigate the Church of the Endtimes and its cultish qualities. The list goes on.

Those are just a few of the "cult" headlines in recent years. You can find others by searching "cult church" on Google News. But the question is, would you recognize a Christian cult if you were in one? Would you know you'd joined a cult before you were effectively brainwashed? How can you discern a Christian cult?

## DISCERNING PROPHETIC CULTS

A wise prophet once said people are destroyed because they lack knowledge (see Hos. 4:6). One of the first steps to deliverance from prophetic cults is arming yourself with the knowledge that helps you discern prophetic cults. If you are in a prophetic cult now, chances are you have a feeling something is wrong but you don't have anyone to talk to about what you are experiencing. That's because, chances are, most of your friends or family are also deceived.

Remember, false prophets work in the realm of lies because they are serving the father of lies. But you are serving the Father of Lights, the Spirit of Truth, and His truth will set you completely free when you embrace it completely (see John 8:32). Decide to be a lover of the truth even if it means admitting you are deceived (see 2 Thess. 2:10). Once you break free, you can help others break free from prophetic cults.

Let's start by defining a cult. *Merriam-Webster*'s dictionary defines *cult* as "a religion regarded as unorthodox or spurious; great devotion to a person, idea, object, movement or work; a system of religious beliefs and ritual." Basically, a prophetic cult is on the fringes of Christianity with strange doctrine that doesn't line up with Scripture. Typically, cults are driven by a key figure or personality, such as Jim Jones at Jonestown or David Koresh in Waco, Texas.

While Scripture doesn't specifically mention prophetic cults, there are many warnings about cult-like figures such as false teachers and false prophets. Paul wrote:

> *For I know this, that after my departure savage wolves will come in among you, not sparing the flock. Also from among yourselves men will rise up, speaking perverse things, to draw away the disciples after themselves. Therefore watch, and remember that for three years I did not cease to warn everyone night and day with tears* (Acts 20:29-31).

Paul was careful not to allow believers to drag him into the cult of personality. He once told the church at Corinth:

> *For where there are envy, strife, and divisions among*
> *you, are you not carnal and behaving like mere men?*
> *For when one says, "I am of Paul," and another, "I am of*
> *Apollos," are you not carnal? Who then is Paul, and who*
> *is Apollos, but ministers through whom you believed, as*
> *the Lord gave to each one? I planted, Apollos watered,*
> *but God gave the increase* (1 Corinthians 3:3-6).

## PROPHETIC CULTS DON'T WANT YOU TO THINK

Prophetic cults have a culture of blind loyalty. Cults propagate thought control. They don't want you to think for yourself or ask questions. This is dangerous. Proverbs tells us, "Only simpletons believe everything they're told!" (Prov. 14:15 NLT). If you can't find something in your Bible, you should question it. If you can't have a healthy discussion with your leader about doctrine, there's a problem.

Deception arises when critical thinking skills are shut down. Paul admonishes us to test all things and hold on to what is good (see 1 Thess. 5:21). He also tells us to detest what is evil and cling to what is good (see Rom. 12:9). Of course, John the apostle said, "Beloved, do not believe every spirit, but test the spirits, whether they are of God; because many false prophets have gone out into the world" (1 John 4:1). All this requires critical thinking and spiritual discernment, which prophetic cults subtly discourage.

Prophetic cults want to shape how you think about other preachers, teachers, prophets, networks, and ministries. They put out reputation hits on those they see as threats. Leaders of these prophetic cults spread rumors and breathe lies against those who see them for who they really are, hoping you will blindly believe them. We need to be good Bereans and search the Scriptures daily to see if what we're being told is true (see Acts 17:11). People are indeed destroyed for lack of Bible knowledge (see Hos. 4:6).

## PROPHETIC CULTS EMPHASIZE BLIND LOYALTY

I'll always remember sitting around a table in an apostle's office with five other staff members. The church was seeing a shaking. Many people were leaving. They had discerned what we had not yet discerned: the church was essentially a prophetic cult. The apostle's wife suddenly announced we were making a lifelong covenant with the apostle, never to leave and always to defend. That meant blind loyalty. I wasn't comfortable when it happened. And most of us who sat around that table finally woke up and left.

Prophetic cults at the extreme will demand you are more loyal to them than to Jesus Himself. I call that toxic loyalty. Scripture says we walk by faith and not by sight, but that doesn't mean we're blind to what defies the Word. Toxic loyalty looks for ways to justify unjustifiable actions. Toxic loyalty causes people to continue to stand by and stand up for people who use and abuse them. Toxic loyalty influences people to give the offender one more chance again and again. Toxic loyalty draws people back into prophetic cults after they've escaped.

Prophetic cult leaders weaponize Scriptures about loyalty, such as Proverbs 21:21 (NASB), "One who pursues righteousness and loyalty finds life, righteousness, and honor." They point to Ruth and Naomi or Moses and Joshua or David and Jonathan as examples of faithfulness, but our faithfulness must be to Jesus first. While loyalty is a godly trait, blind loyalty can be the snare of witchcraft. Oswald Chambers once said, "Beware of anything that competes with your loyalty to Jesus Christ." Wise words. We are supposed to hold fast to Jesus (see Col. 2:19).

## PROPHETIC CULTS MOVE IN FALSE REVELATION

Prophetic cults thrive on secret knowledge and special revelations. That's not surprising, given the definition of *occult*. According to *Merriam-Webster*'s dictionary, *occult* means "to shut off from view or exposure: secret; not easily apprehended or understood; mysterious; matters regarded as involving the action or influence of supernatural or supernormal powers or some secret knowledge of them."

Look at Jim Jones, David Koresh, or Marshall Applewhite. They all claimed special revelations that completely contradicted Scripture. While we value the prophetic and supernatural encounters with God, too much focus on these without the truth as an anchor can lead us into deceptive waters.

## PROPHETIC CULTS MOVE IN SPIRITUAL ERROR

Prophetic cults form around error. Of course, prophetic cults aren't always as dramatic as Jonestown. The problem is, spiritual error sounds good and right to the hungry heart that isn't rooted and grounded in the Word. One example—and this one is purposely far out to make a point—is an overemphasis on strange manifestations of the Holy Spirit. I'm not against unusual manifestations, but when we emphasize the manifestations over Jesus we get in trouble. And sometimes the manifestations are anything but holy.

Please don't get me wrong. I am all for experiencing the authentic power of God. I am all for valid manifestations of the Holy Spirit. I believe in the gifts of the Spirit. I love to witness signs, wonders, and miracles. I expect to see more of that in the days ahead. But I am concerned that some are ill-equipped to discern the difference between the Spirit of God and strange fire.

I've been to prayer meetings where a woman's eyes were rolling into the back of her head and her eyelids were fluttering rapidly as if she was under demonic control. (Are you going to tell me that the Holy Spirit rolls your eyes in the back of your head when you pray in the Spirit?) During service I saw that same woman up on the platform singing, then she abruptly stopped worshiping to prophesy utter nonsense for 10 minutes. The pastor did nothing.

I've seen people "toking" imaginary marijuana cigarettes and passing it down the line as if the Holy Ghost is some sort of drug. Again the pastor did nothing. People meow like cats, grown men lay on the floor in a sweaty huddle for hours, either unconscious or in some sort of funky haze, and teenagers twitch and shake uncontrollably as if having a seizure. I am aware of the Quakers, but this is far beyond that.

Again, I'm all for genuine manifestations of the Holy Spirit and I've participated in plenty of them. But I never read about Abel's eyes rolling in the back of his head when he brought his offering to

God. There isn't anything in the Bible about Enoch's eyes fluttering rapidly and uncontrollably as he was raptured. Noah wasn't passing imaginary joints to his family in the ark. Abraham didn't have pile-ups with the 318 men trained in his own house. The Bible doesn't record Isaac, Jacob, or Joseph meowing like cats (or even barking like dogs or hissing like snakes). Moses didn't shake and twitch uncontrollably for an hour as if having epileptic seizure when he saw the glory of God.

If these heroes of faith didn't record such strange manifestations of the Spirit of God, how can we be so quick to say it's the Spirit of God? Can we automatically endorse hissing, writhing, and barking just because John said many things Jesus did weren't recorded in the Bible? Shouldn't we test the spirits, like the Bible says?

At the end of the day, I look at Jesus. You don't get any fuller of the Holy Spirit than Jesus. And I never saw my Jesus rolling around on the ground pretending to smoke imaginary weed or rolling His eyes in the back of His head or making animal noises. I haven't seen one record of Spirit-filled saints acting that way in the Bible. You would think if such mad manifestations were genuinely of the Holy Spirit and fell on those who were desperately seeking God's face, we would see them recorded in the Book of Acts. Yes, we see strange miracles, but that didn't include hissing, barking, writhing, etc.

I believe an unbalanced pursuit of supernatural experiences opens the door to demon-inspired encounters and emotions that validate a person's erroneous theology. Some in the prophetic movement claim to hold regular conversations with angels, which become the source of their prophecies and sermons. Yes, angels are prophetic messengers, but most often the Holy Spirit will lead us and guide us into all truth Himself. And our sermons should be based on the Word of God—and our prophecies from the Spirit of God—not mystical revelation that doesn't line up with the Bible.

Chasing the supernatural above the God of the supernatural is not the only example of emotionalism gone amuck. The prosperity gospel can also get out of balance. I've read about merchandising evangelists leading people into financial devastation after a so-called supernatural promise that gave them false faith to believe their debt would be canceled in thirty days. Yes, I believe in supernatural debt cancellation, but there is an abuse of these truths and it can become a profitable gimmick. People fall for it because they are in their emotions rather than in the Word of God. They tap into the hype and the shyster taps into their pocketbooks.

## PROPHETIC CULTS ISOLATE YOU FROM OTHERS

When I was part of the cultish church I mentioned, I had to ask permission to go home for Christmas. A friend of mine had to ask permission to get married. Prophetic cults work to isolate you—cutting you off from family and friends who might discern what is really going on.

You may have heard of controlling churches with an approved reading list or a blacklist. The leaders are working to control what you read. It's one thing to try to protect your church or network by warning them of materials that contain error. It's another thing altogether to keep them from healthy content or ministries that will fuel their spiritual life. Proverbs 18:1 tells us when we isolate ourselves we rage against sound wisdom.

## PROPHETIC CULTS ENGAGE IN SPIRITUAL ABUSE

Prophetic cult leaders don't always operate like Jim Jones. Controlling ministries tend to hide behind the guise of spiritual coverings. And far too many outsiders are not willing to even question the messages and practices of such churches. It takes lovers of truth with spiritual discernment to recognize the sometimes-subtle signs of abusive churches. And it takes courage to confront it.

What exactly is spiritual abuse? Jeff VanVonderen, co-author of the classic book *The Subtle Power of Spiritual Abuse*, explains it this way: "Spiritual abuse occurs when someone in a position of spiritual authority...misuses that authority placing themselves over God's people to control, coerce or manipulate them for seemingly godly purposes which are really their own."[1]

Spiritual abuse is hardly a new phenomenon. You can find instances in the Bible of spiritual leaders exploiting people to build their kingdoms. In Jeremiah 8, the Lord called out the abuse of prophets and priests, saying, "They dress the wound of my people as though it were not serious" (Jer. 8:11 NIV). The root problems of people in the "church" were treated superficially. In other words, the pastor put a Band-Aid on the problem so things looked good from the outside but the wound was festering on the inside. The pastor's prominence was more important than the legitimate needs of the congregation.

Today, this manifests as spiritual leaders recruiting volunteers to build their ministries while neglecting to minister to the real needs of hurting people. In such cases, churches become like businesses. The pastor is more like a CEO than a spiritual leader. Staff meetings center on marketing initiatives that will bring more people—who will bring more tithes and offerings—into the sanctuary. Church services become about external appearances, but the whitewashed tombs are full of dead men's bones.

Jesus addressed spiritual abuse in His day. Beyond His warnings about the Pharisees, Jesus also pointed out ravenous wolves. These ravenous wolves look much like anointed prophets, but their motives are dastardly. Today, the spiritually abusive pharisaical pastor has a long list of rules and demands and little grace for those who don't rise to the occasion.

Entire books have been written on spiritual abuse. Those books will help you see spiritual abuse for what it is, how you got sucked into the cycle, how to break free from spiritual abuse, and how to recover from spiritual abuse once you've escaped its clutches. But for now, I want to leave you with some nuggets from Dave Johnson and Jeff VanVonderen's book, *The Subtle Power of Spiritual Abuse*.

*Power-posturing is a telltale sign of spiritual abuse.* Power-posturing leaders spend a lot of time focused on their own authority and reminding others of it. Johnson and VanVonderen say this is necessary because their spiritual authority isn't real—based on genuine godly character—it is postured.

In practical terms, this might manifest as a leader who likes to remind the congregation that he can excommunicate people or that any anointing you are flowing in comes from the head (meaning him, not Jesus). This leader can never be questioned, and is usually not accountable to anyone. Those around him are usually mere "yes men" who do his bidding in exchange for delegated authority to lord over others.

Performance preoccupation is a sign of spiritual abuse. Johnson and VanVonderen note that obedience and submission are two important words often used in abusive church structures.

Don't get me wrong. Obedience and submission are important. But spiritual abuse often shames or scares people into obedience and submission. True obedience is a matter of the heart. Spiritual abusers apply undue pressure that is not from God. That pressure is usually applied to get you to do the leader's will, not God's will.

*Unspoken rules are common in instances of spiritual abuse.* "In abusive spiritual systems," Johnson and VanVonderen offer, "people's lives are controlled from the outside in by rules, spoken and unspoken."

"Unspoken rules are those that govern unhealthy churches or families but are not said out loud. Because they are not said out loud, you don't find out that they're there until you break them,"[2] Johnson and VanVonderen write. It often seems these "rules" hold more power than Scripture.

The "Can't Talk" rule is seen where spiritual abuse is present. Johnson and VanVonderen explain that the "can't talk" rule blames the person who talks, and the ensuing punishments pressure questioners into silence.

If you voice a problem you become the problem. If you question why the church no longer picks up the poor kids in the ministry van but has shifted its focus to more affluent neighborhoods, you are removed from your role as a volunteer driver. Others see your fate and decide they'd better not rock the boat. It's a form of intimidation.

*Lack of balance and extremism is often present where spiritual abuse lives.* This manifests as an unbalanced approach to living out the truth of the Christian life. Johnson and VanVonderen explain that in these systems it is more important to act according to the word of a leader who has "a word" for you than to act according to what you know to be true from Scripture or simply from your spiritual-growth history.

The truth is prophetic words don't carry the same weight as Scripture, and you can hear from God for yourself. When you rely on other people to tell you what God is saying, you open the door to control and manipulation.

It's not possible to fully expose the inner workings of spiritual abuse, Christian cults, and controlling churches in a single article. My goal is to raise awareness of a troubling issue and get you thinking—not to send you on a witch hunt for spiritual abusers.

If you think you are part of a spiritually abusive cult-like or controlling church, ask the Lord to break any deception off your mind and show you the truth. The truth could be that you are in a healthy church and you just need to die to self. But it could be that you are in an abusive system and you need to break free. If your heart is purely seeking the truth, the Holy Spirit will surely guide you there (see John 16:13).

## DON'T GO ON A WITCH HUNT

Just because you don't agree with a ministry's doctrine doesn't make that ministry a cult. In eternity, I imagine we'll discover no single denomination or ministry had the interpretation of every jot and tittle one hundred percent accurate one hundred percent of the time. There's a difference between honest error and a spirit of error.

Some theological points are worth debating. If a church denies the deity of Christ, for example, I'd call it a cult or a false religion. Scripture is crystal clear that Jesus is the Son of God. There is no wiggle room for misinterpreting that one. But differences in other theological points, such as the rapture or end times, are not as crystal clear. There is so much symbology that well-respected ministries come to different conclusions about what the Bible says regarding the rapture or eternity. I wouldn't label a ministry as a cult just because I don't absolutely agree with their end-times theology.

There are many different theologies in the Body of Christ. As a Christian, you can't possibly agree with them all. But that doesn't mean everyone who doesn't agree with you is a cult. In fact, one of the earmarks of cultish thinking is the attitude that you are the only one who has the truth on a matter of Scripture.

Paul told Timothy to avoid foolish and ignorant disputes, knowing that they generate strife (see 2 Tim. 2:23). *The Message* Bible puts it this way: "Refuse to get involved in inane discussions; they always end up in fights." And the Amplified Bible, Classic Edition says "refuse (shut your mind against, have nothing to do with) trifling (ill-informed, unedifying, stupid) controversies over ignorant questionings, for you know that they foster strife and breed quarrels."

To be sure, calling a ministry a cult is an extremely serious allegation. Yet every major ministry has witnessed this persecution. Kenneth Hagin has been accused of leading a cult. Joyce Meyer has been called a heretic. John Hagee has been deemed the leader of the "Left Behind Cult." Would you believe that Billy Graham had even been accused of cult association? The list goes on and on.

I've armed you with information on how to identify a cult, but, please, be careful not to go on a witch hunt. Don't be one of those cheesy heresy hunters on YouTube who take a prophet's words out of context and paint him to be false when it's only a matter of debatable theology. Remember, as I said in my book *The Making of a Watchman*, be a watchman, not a watchdog:

> Positioning yourself as a watchdog instead of a watchman can be tempting if you don't know how to deal with righteous indignation over errors (or what you perceive as errors) you see in the Body of Christ. Watchdogs behave more like dogs that guard a property. They bark at everyone who approaches whether good or bad. A watchdog is typically self-appointed. There are secular watchdogs and spiritual watchdogs. But most watchdogs are not tamed and they can easily slide over into the realm of heresy hunter. Watchdogs may carry a spirit of control or a spirit of criticism or even a spirit of suspicion rather than discernment.[3]

You don't want to become like the thing you hate.

# NOTES

1. David Johnson and Jeff VanVonderen, *The Subtle Power of Spiritual Abuse* (Bloomington, MN: Bethany House Publishers, 1991), 13.

2. Ibid., 67.

3. Jennifer LeClaire, *The Making of a Watchman* (Shippensburg, PA: Destiny Image Publishers, 2021), 165.

# CHAPTER 4

# DELIVERANCE FROM FALSE
# PROPHETIC
# SOUL TIES

I was saved in a county jail after being imprisoned for a crime I did not commit. I was there for forty days and, thanks be to Jesus, I got radically saved. After I became a bondservant for Christ, God vindicated me and I walked out a free woman in more ways than one. Unfortunately, though I became rich in Christ, I was dirt poor in the natural. I spent all the money I had on the attorney who defended my innocence.

When I got out of jail, my parents had already forfeited my apartment and gotten rid of my dog. So now I was homeless, without money and without a job (or a dog). It was miserable living with my parents, so I moved to a small town in Alabama to rebuild my life. After thirteen months, God sent me back to South Florida to reoccupy the land.

My first order of business was to enroll my daughter in kindergarten. My second goal was to find a Spirit-filled church. It didn't take me long to find a church that was within just a couple of miles from my house. I felt so blessed. Much of the teaching was new to me, but it was exciting and I was learning and growing so quickly. I made a friend there, Jackie, who was the administrator of the church. She was passionate about God.

I started volunteering in that church immediately and since Jackie was over the volunteers, we had a lot of opportunity to get to know each other and spend time doing the Lord's work together. We hit it off, and she became a huge help in so many ways. Since I had a five-year-old daughter (and was a single mother) I needed all the help I could get. And since she was saved longer than me, she encouraged me in the Word. It seemed like a divine connection—and I believe it was. A healthy soul tie was formed—until it all turned toxic.

When she came under the spell of our toxic church leader—serving as his eunuch, his puppet, his hitman—I became the victim of her delegated power. He was controlling her, and she then set out to control me for his sake so she would not endure his wrath. Essentially, without realizing it, I had a soul tie with Jezebel. Well, not exactly with Jezebel; with Jackie, who was under the influence of a Jezebel spirit. Because I was so young in the Lord, I didn't know she had a Jezebel spirit and I didn't know what a soul tie was, which put me at a double disadvantage.

Being ignorant of the devil's devices always makes us a target. Other people—even people in the church we both attended—tried to tell me she had gone off the deep end. But I didn't see it at first. I didn't want to see it. Eventually I could not ignore it. The last straw was her secret marriage to another leader in the church—a marriage the lead pastors covered up. That secret wedding was followed months later by a fancy public wedding and then a third wedding—a church wedding—for those not invited to the fancy wedding. This was deceit and narcissism at its best. My eyes were then wide open and it was heartbreaking to see all the deception.

## WHAT IS A SOUL TIE?

The Bible doesn't use the phrase "soul tie," but it is a biblical concept. A soul tie is a special connection between two people. It's a bond. It's a deeply spiritual and emotional connection. A soul tie can be healthy or toxic. And a soul tie can compel you to act in ways that are selfless—and at times well beyond your best interests when they sour.

Healthy soul ties may look like the bond between a mother and a child, a brother and a sister, a husband and a wife—or best friends. But soul ties can also be extremely dangerous, such as between an abuser and his punching bag or a stalker and his victim. Soul ties can start out healthy and become toxic or they can be toxic from the start.

Biblically, we see the concept of a soul tie in 1 Samuel 18:1-4:

> *Now when he had finished speaking to Saul, the soul of Jonathan was knit to the soul of David, and Jonathan loved him as his own soul. Saul took him that*

*day, and would not let him go home to his father's house anymore. Then Jonathan and David made a covenant, because he loved him as his own soul. And Jonathan took off the robe that was on him and gave it to David, with his armor, even to his sword and his bow and his belt.*

## UNDERSTANDING THE GENESIS OF SOUL TIES

You may be wondering how soul ties form. It's a need-to-know question. There are at least four ways soul ties can form. As mentioned, the first is close relationships, like that of a mother and child or friends like Jonathan and David. We also see the hint of a soul tie in Genesis 44.

After Joseph ascended as prime minister of Egypt, his brothers came looking for food in the famine. Joseph sent them home with food in their sacks and their money on top of the grain. But Joseph also set them up for a fall by putting his silver cup in the mouth of Benjamin's bag. Long story short, Joseph sent someone after his brothers to accuse them of stealing his cup. The brothers knew they had not taken the cup and agreed that whoever had the cup would be Joseph's slave. Shortly after, they found the cup in Benjamin's bag, Joseph's whole brother and Jacob's youngest son.

Finding the cup in Benjamin's bag was devastating. Judah, one of Joseph's brothers, pleaded with him not to keep Benjamin behind. Judah pleaded, "Now therefore, when I come to your servant my father, and the lad is not with us, since his life is bound up in the lad's life, it will happen, when he sees that the lad is not with us, that he will die" (Gen. 44:30-31).

Can you see it? When you have a soul tie, your life is tied up in another person's life. What many people don't realize is you can have soul ties with churches, coworkers, classmates, networks, and preachers you don't even know personally. Jezebel's prophets work to create a soul tie with you, but they aren't as invested in you as you are in them. They just want you to be dependent on them. Yes, a soul tie can be one-sided.

A soul tie can also form during sexual relations when two become one flesh—or even through emotional affairs. That's why it's not wise for a man to share intimate details of his life with a woman who is not his wife (and vice versa). In an emotional affair, a person may feel closer to the outsider than to his own spouse. That may eventually lead to sexual relations. Paul the apostle said when a man and wife are joined, the two become one flesh (see Eph. 5:31).

And it's not just with your spouse. Paul also said, "Or do you not know that he who is joined to a harlot is one body with her? For 'the two,' He says, 'shall become one flesh'" (1 Cor. 6:16). The University of Seattle and the Fred Hutchinson Cancer Research Centre discovered in a study that women carry living DNA from all the men they have had a sexual relationship with. That's why you need to break unhealthy soul ties with anyone with whom you've had sexual intercourse.

Soul ties are one reason why divorces and breakups are so difficult. Physical, mental, and emotional soul ties are severed in the natural by legal orders or distance. But many people don't realize these soul ties must also be severed in the spirit. If you don't break the soul ties, they act as a magnet that holds you to the past. You may grieve longer than you should or keep trying to work the relationship out even though it's toxic.

## SPIRITUAL CONTRACTS WITH DEMONS

A soul tie can form when you make vows to or covenants with someone. Consider Numbers 30:1-2 (NIV), "This is what the Lord commands: When a man makes a vow to the Lord or takes an oath to obligate himself by a pledge, he must not break his word but must do everything he said."

The enemy also works to enforce vows. When you pledge, "I will never leave this church" or "I will never stop loving you," you are not only making a covenant with a person, you are also making an inner vow. I talk more about these spiritual contracts in my series *Spiritual Contracts* at www.schoolofthespirit.tv/contracts. Be careful not to enter covenant relationships too quickly.

You can even unknowingly make vows with spirits by saying things like, "I'll never let anyone hurt me like that again" or "I will always protect my back from now on." In fact, when you say such words, the spirit of Jezebel (and other spirits) hears you and sees it as an invitation to provide perverted protection by coming to your defense when you face unfair treatment.

When you feel wronged, you may tend to manifest self-preserving behavior that's literally influenced by God's spiritual enemies. This is sinful in many ways, but mostly because we are supposed to trust in the Lord with all our hearts—not lean to our own understanding or lean on a demon power to protect us. If you have a soul tie with someone operating in a Jezebel or Ahab spirit, it is difficult to resist their influence in your life. You have to break the soul tie.

A soul tie is different from a curse in that you entered into it willingly, in most cases, even if it was unknowingly. The exception on the sexual front would be rape. People who are kidnapped often form soul ties with their captors, but these types of situations are not typical to most people. Most people enter into soul ties willfully, again, even if they don't realize it.

## SIGNS OF TOXIC SOUL TIES

So how would you know if you have a toxic soul tie? You may have already discerned it, which is why you are reading this book. Or you may still not be sure because deception is clouding your mind. But, if you are still reading intently, you may be discerning something in your present or past that is troubling you.

First, understand there can be physical soul ties, emotional soul ties, spiritual soul ties, and social soul ties. For purposes of prophetic witchcraft, we're dealing primary with spiritual soul ties, but you may have several forms of soul ties with one person or organization. Yes, you can have a soul tie with a group or church.

You know you have a soul tie due to the deep connection you have with a person, place, or thing. You feel drawn to them despite any drama. The person you're soul tied to knows how to push your buttons. They know what makes you tick. You know you have a soul tie because you are also familiar with their ways. You may be able to complete their sentences or just know what they are thinking before they even say it. Your guard is down when you are around them because you feel safe, or at least you used to before the soul tie became toxic.

When you have a soul tie you can't bring yourself to cut off the relationship even though you can clearly see it's unhealthy or even abusive. You justify their actions or second guess if you're discerning correctly. You don't want to believe the relationship is toxic. It took me two years to break a toxic soul tie with a church. It took me two years to break a toxic soul tie with a company. The only way one typically breaks a soul tie is when the pain of the connection becomes greater than the pain of breaking the connection.

If you feel like you need someone's approval to try to do something new in your life, you may have a toxic soul tie. I am not talking about discussing plans with your spouse or even a friend. I am talking about a fear of upsetting them or being the victim of anger or abuse. If you take on another person's offenses, that's a sure sign of a toxic soul tie. You can even be offended for the person with whom you have a soul tie when they are not offended themselves.

Depending on the depth of the soul tie, you may even take on another person's mood. When your mood shifts dramatically because someone else is moody—say anger or depression—that's a sign that you have an emotional instability. While we are supposed to rejoice with those who rejoice and weep with those who weep, we are not supposed to be influenced deeply by the toxic emotions of others. If your mood depends on someone else's mood, you may have a soul tie. If you feel like the person with whom you have a soul tie is watching you, it's toxic. If you can't reason for yourself, if you feel controlled and manipulated in the relationship but bow to them anyway, or if you feel used in the relationship, you may have a toxic soul tie.

If you stalk someone on social media, you may have a toxic soul tie. If you are compelled to find out where someone is, what they are doing, if they are talking about you, or who they are talking to, it's not a healthy dynamic. If you ignore warnings from family and friends to break ties even though you know something is wrong, you probably have a toxic soul tie. If you frequently compromise your values or standards to accommodate the relationship, it's definitely a toxic soul tie. If you are confused about the relationship, miserable in the relationship, or tormented in any way because of the relationship, the soul tie is toxic.

If you break off physical contact with a person or place but feel drawn back to them or can't seem to get them out of your mind, that's a clear sign of a toxic soul tie. When they call you, you are tempted to pick up the phone and may even converse with them. The temptation to shut them completely out may be too much and you may continue to let them in from time to time, only to see more clearly how toxic the situation really is.

## PREPARING TO SEVER THE TIES

If you've discerned you have a toxic soul tie, don't fret. You can choose by the force of your will to break the soul tie. It takes some preparation. For example, you may have to enter into forgiveness first for the place or person who has held you back and held you down for the sake of their own pleasure or advancement.

Once you see how toxic the relationship was, you may get very angry. Paul wrote, "'Be angry, and do not sin': do not let the sun go down on your wrath, nor give place to the devil" (Eph. 4:26-27).

God wants to set a table before you in the presence of your enemies, but if you give place to the devil God will have to wait until you obey His command to forgive. If you don't forgive, you won't be able to walk in your God-given authority.

You also need to get rid of anything in your possession connected with the one with whom you are breaking an ungodly soul tie. This could mean photographs, gifts, jewelry, clothing items—anything that ties you to that person. I know that sounds extreme, especially if the items are expensive. But any reminder can open the door to voices of the past and draw you back. Nothing is worth your freedom. Visible memories can drive you into double-mindedness. You want to be sober-minded, not double-minded. Check out my book *Cleansing Your Home from Evil* as a supplement.

By the same token, if you've made any vows under your breath like the ones I described—"I'll never let anyone hurt me again!"—repent of them right now. Even vows to people like, "I will never leave this church" or "I will love you to the end of time" need to be broken if they are spoken rashly or in the midst of a sinful relationship. Just say, "I break every inner vow I made claiming _____, in Jesus' name."

You may even find yourself disillusioned with God over the trauma, but remember: it wasn't God's fault. He tried to warn you of the danger. He may have even sent others, like family or friends, to warn you. Somehow, you missed the warning or maybe even ignored it. Nothing is ever God's fault. He loves you. Finally, forgive yourself. If you are harboring unforgiveness toward yourself, you will not break free from soul ties. Unforgiveness is unforgiveness.

## BREAKING TOXIC SOUL TIES

Breaking a soul tie is not difficult. It starts with repentance. You need to turn the other way. You need to change the way you think. If you have committed some manner of sin that led you into a soul tie—such as sexual sin—renounce and repent of the offense and ask God for forgiveness. I know I am asking you to do some hard things, but there's no condemnation in Christ Jesus (see Rom. 8:1). You need to engage in godly sorrow, true and deep repentance that will completely break you free from every tie that binds. Paul put it this way in 2 Corinthians 7:8-12:

> For even if I made you sorry with my letter, I do not regret it; though I did regret it. For I perceive that the same epistle made you sorry, though only for a while. Now I rejoice, not that you were made sorry, but that your sorrow led to repentance. For you were made sorry in a godly manner, that you might suffer loss from us in nothing. For godly sorrow produces repentance leading to salvation, not to be regretted; but the sorrow of the world produces death.
>
> For observe this very thing, that you sorrowed in a godly manner: What diligence it produced in you, what clearing of yourselves, what indignation, what fear, what vehement desire, what zeal, what vindication! In all things you proved yourselves to be clear in this matter. Therefore, although I wrote to you, I did not do it for the sake of him who had done the wrong, nor for the sake of him who suffered wrong, but that our care for you in the sight of God might appear to you.

Do you see it? Godly sorrow drives breakthrough. Now you can break the toxic soul tie. Here's an example prayer: "I renounce this soul tie with Jamie, in the name of Jesus. I want no part of this ungodly soul tie. I sever it right now and plead the blood of Jesus over my mind and mouth. I repent of the sin that led me into this soul tie. I forgive the ones I have tied myself to, I ask You to forgive them and me, and I forgive myself." You can elaborate on this phrase with more descriptors and sincerity, but these are the elements you need to address when breaking soul ties.

## BUILDING DIVINE CONNECTIONS

Don't just stop there. Renew your mind with the Word of God. Study what true, healthy relationships look like and pursue them. Don't allow the enemy to keep you from engaging with people and organizations just because you got burned. The enemy wants to isolate you. God will lead you to divine connections. Divine connections—those God-breathed relationships that seemingly come out of nowhere and have the potential to radically impact your life—are vital.

It's critical that we distinguish between a divine connection and a soul tie. Remember, a soul tie is when hearts are knitted together. Hearts can be knitted together in true love, which is what Paul talks about in Colossians 2:2. That's a healthy soul tie. All soul ties are not divine connections, though. Soul ties can form through carnal or demonic connections. So then, what does a divine connection look like?

Divine connections bear fruit just like carnal or demonic connections. So first, be a fruit inspector. Divine connections will bear divine fruit. Divine connections advance God's will for your life. Divine connections encourage you when you are down and help you see what you can't see. Divine connections forward your purpose or God-given assignment in any given season. Divine connections may be problem solvers in your life or open doors of opportunity that you can't open. As I wrote in my book *Walking in Your Prophetic Destiny*:

> A divine connection may not always be a close personal relationship. It could be a door-opener relationship. I've experienced too many of these divine connections to count. These could be long-term or short-term relationships—so short-term in fact that you never see that divine connection again—sort of like that mystery person who picks up your dinner check in a restaurant. In this context, God gives you supernatural favor with people in positions of authority and power who can open a door He wants opened with the Isaiah 22:22 key. I would not be where I am today without door-opener connections.
>
> A divine connection can manifest in the form of an intercessor on whom God has laid a burden to pray. Although I often say I don't have enough intercession to adequately cover my ministry, God has used divine connection intercessors in my life at strategic times to blast through demonic opposition to birthing my next assignment. In this way, divine intercessors can clear the path to divine appointments—and other divine connections.

A divine connection can also connect you to resources you need to advance your prophetic destiny—whether that's money, information, or revelation. I've enjoyed divine connection prophets in my life who have given me a word in due season that explained things I could not see. I've appreciated divine connection financiers who have helped me fund various ministry projects. God owns the cattle on a thousand hills (Psalm 50:10). The silver is His. The gold is His. He is all-knowing, all-seeing, all-mighty, and all-sufficient.[1]

## NOTE

1. Jennifer LeClaire, *Walking in Your Prophetic Destiny* (Nashville, TN: Thomas Nelson, 2019), 135-136.

CHAPTER 5

# DELIVERANCE FROM FALSE
# PROPHETIC
# OPERATIONS

I've seen false prophets all-out humiliate people or even curse them in the name of Jesus. Many years ago, I was part of a church where the apostle invited in a visiting minister from Europe. He boldly (and rather proudly) announced to us all that God had promoted him from pastor to prophet after years of faithful service. That was the first red flag for me. God doesn't promote you on a sliding scale into new anointings based on tenure in the Kingdom. Mantles and anointings can grow and shift—God can reveal gifts and graces that were always in you that are more fully activated at the opportune time—but we aren't promoted into new offices based on length of service.

Sitting on the front row, I watched for hours as this pastor prophesied over 100 or more people one by one in depth. I heard most of it because he was speaking into the microphone. I was beyond grieved. It seems God must have been in a bad mood that day and wanted to embarrass and tear down everyone in the prayer line. (Of course, God was not in a bad mood, but the prophet was in bad form.) One by one, people left the prayer line covered in prophetic witchcraft.

Finally, it was my turn to receive a prophetic word from this wayward "prophet." I didn't want to go up to the prayer line because I knew what would happen. I knew he would curse me. But church leadership demanded cooperation. If we didn't go up it would look like we didn't trust the newly minted "prophet," and the apostle was more concerned with impressing the minister than protecting his flock.

I was young in the Lord then and didn't have the boldness to reject the instruction, and it was to my demise. The so-called prophet started prophesying profusely that I was emotionally unstable and struggled in my faith. My eyes started to burn and I started to feel a heavy weight on me. Even though what he said wasn't true and the fruit of my life defied the word, I suddenly felt ashamed and wanted to hide.

## A WITCH IN THE HOUSE

Unfortunately, this was not my only experience with prophetic witchcraft. But the incident with the European prophet prepared me for another troubling encounter many years ago. We invited a prophet to Awakening House of Prayer. He seemed fine on the outside. Many people were inviting him to speak. He was in all the popular prophetic magazines. From the outside looking in, everything seemed legit.

At the end of his message, he started preaching something that hit my spirit wrong. I couldn't put my finger on it. But it wasn't quite right. Those around me started looking over because they also picked up something was off. It was subtle at first and hard to believe, but it was there to discern. This prophet made an altar call and many people went up for prayer at our conference.

When I went home, I prayed and asked the Lord what was going on. He said it was prophetic witchcraft and not to let this man teach again the next day. It was extremely awkward, to say the least, because he was supposed to share another message and I didn't know how I was going to graciously stop him. To be sure, it was the most awkward situation I was ever in, but I knew I could not allow him back into my pulpit. I was going to call him and release him from the assignment because he had some issue back home he was trying to deal with, but he showed up at the church extra early—before I could call.

I was asking the Lord for wisdom and decided to let the worship team worship for an hour or so and then pray. But when I showed up, the worship leader had no voice. She had been hit with prophetic witchcraft. I grabbed two women from the congregation to sing. During worship, I was led to ask how many in the church had nightmares, sickness, or other attacks overnight. To a person, everyone who had been prayed for at the altar the night before raised their hands. I spent the next hour breaking witchcraft off them. I had to repent to the Lord for not discerning the prophetic witchcraft on this man and inviting him in—and letting him pray for anyone.

Be careful not to just run up to any prayer line, even when, or should I say, especially when the preacher is prophesying over everything that moves. If you know them and their reputation, you are on safe ground. True prophets do get in flows where they can prophesy for hours on end accurately. But if you don't know this person, don't be too quick to open your soul to their prophetic words or you could be the victim of witchcraft. Again, if you face prophetic witchcraft you need break the words over your life—immediately. Don't wait.

## BREAKING FALSE PROPHETIC WORDS

Now let's go back to the moment when the prophet from Europe released those evil words over me. Being so young in the Lord, I didn't know what to do. I had to go to the other prophets in the church and ask for help. They discerned it was witchcraft and prayed to break it. We later went to the apostle explaining how out of order we sensed this "prophet" was, and he verbally scourged us and punished us. I continue to say that the prophetic word you don't judge is the prophetic word that can derail your life—at least for a season. We need to judge prophecy before we accept it as true and wage war with it according to 1 Timothy 1:18.

When you receive a prophetic word that doesn't bear witness with your spirit, there are times to put it on the shelf and wait and see if it comes to pass. However, when a word hits your spirit wrong you should not just let that word linger over your life waiting for an opportunity to manifest. The false prophetic word may have been innocently released, but that doesn't mean it can't wreak havoc on your life. By the same token, the prophetic word may have been malicious. Either way, the words must be broken.

A perverse prophetic word can break the spirit (see Prov. 15:4). The word *perverse* in that text comes from the Greek word *celeph*. According to *The KJV Old Testament Hebrew Lexicon*, it means "crookedness, perverseness, or crooked dealing." God will use true prophecy as one way to make the crooked places straight in your life. The enemy uses false prophecy to make the straight places crooked. Don't let him.

Likewise, we know that words can defile a person (see Matt. 15:18). When you pray through and war with a false prophetic word—when you confess it, agree with it, and meditate on it—it can defile you. *Defile* means to corrupt. The enemy wants to bring corruption in your life through false prophecy, corrupting your mind, will, emotions, imaginations, reasoning, and intellect. He wants to renew your mind to the wrong word. Don't let him.

Jesus said His words are spirit and life (see John 6:63). In the same way, the enemy's words are spirit and death. Whomever we agree with will escort us into our next season; as Amos 3:3 tells us plainly, two can't walk together unless they agree. When you agree with false prophecy, you may very well be disagreeing with God's true word over your life by default—even if it's in ignorance. That's why Paul warns us not be ignorant of the devil's devices (see 2 Cor. 2:11).

On top of that, faith comes by hearing (see Rom. 10:17). When we hear a true prophecy, it's wrapped in the faith we need to believe it. When we hear a false prophecy, it can build faith in a lie if we willingly receive it. Sometimes, we put so much trust in prophets we don't think twice about judging the prophetic word. And that's one way the enemy steals, kills, and destroys. (I wrote about judging prophecy in the first book in this trilogy, *Discerning Prophetic Witchcraft*.)

So what is the answer? We need to cast down the false prophecy just like we'd cast down an imagination. Paul wrote, "Casting down arguments and every high thing that exalts itself against the knowledge of God, bringing every thought into captivity to the obedience of Christ" (2 Cor. 10:5). Pray this way: "I cast down this false prophecy. I break the powers of every false spirit, false word, and error spoken over my life, in Jesus' name. I declare every false word over my life will fall to the ground and no weapon of false prophecy formed against me will prevail."

## BREAKING PROPHETIC WORD CURSES

I sat under a toxic apostle who prophesied in anger that anyone who left his church would wander around without an anointing. This defies Scripture, seeing as John told us we have an anointing from the Holy One (see 1 John 2:20). Nevertheless, this apostle said any anointing we thought we had came from him. That's heresy. Later, the prophet of the house said I would never fit into any other church. These were prophetic curses.

Some people don't take prophetic word curses seriously because the Bible says the curse causeless shall not come (see Prov. 26:2). That's a mistake. It's interesting to break down what that really means. According to The *KJV Old Testament Hebrew Lexicon*, *curse* means "curse, vilification, execration." The first definition of *curse*, according to *Merriam-Webster*, means "a prayer or invocation for harm or injury to come upon one."

*Causeless* in Proverbs 26:2 comes from the Hebrew word *chinnam*. One of *The KJV Old Testament Hebrew Lexicon* definitions of this word is "for no purpose." Every curse carries a purpose. A curse of poverty intends to see its victim poor. A curse of sickness intends to see its victim infirmed. A curse of death intends to see its victim dead. Just as blessings are wrapped in faith, I believe curses are wrapped in fear. *Come* in this verse is the Hebrew word *bow*. One of the definitions points to an enemy attack. So we see the curse is an attack that purposes to bring harm or injury.

Proverbs 18:21 declares, "Death and life are in the power of the tongue." We curse, primarily, with our tongues. Christians can release curses against you. Witches can release curses against you. You can release curses against yourself. Yes, you can release prophetic witchcraft at yourself. Here's the disturbing part: according to the *International Standard Bible Encyclopedia*, "A curse was considered to possess an inherent power of carrying itself into effect."

## JEZEBEL CURSED ELIJAH—AND HERSELF

Jezebel released a prophetic word curse against Elijah:

> *Then Jezebel sent a messenger to Elijah, saying, "So may the gods do to me and even more, if I do not make your life as the life of one of them by tomorrow about this time." And he was afraid and arose and ran for his*

*life and came to Beersheba, which belongs to Judah,*
*and left his servant there* (1 Kings 19:2-3 NASB95).

Word curses from authority figures in our lives seem to carry more weight because we put more stock in them—we are more likely to accept their words. But once we see the person as false, it strips away much of the power. We strip away the rest through prayer. A false prophet launched a curse at one of my spiritual sons, for example, swearing his ministry would fail in ninety days if he didn't return to the network. The curse fell to the ground but not without a lot of offensive warfare tactics to prevent the curse from bringing itself to pass.

Proverbs 12:18 (JUB) reveals there are those who "speak like the piercings of a sword." Proverbs 15:4 (MEV) tells us, "A wholesome tongue is a tree of life, but perverseness in it crushes the spirit." Proverbs 11:9 (MEV) reveals, "A hypocrite with his mouth destroys his neighbor, but through knowledge the just will be delivered." And Proverbs 25:18 says, "A man who bears false witness against his neighbor is like a club, a sword, and a sharp arrow."

James 3:8 tells us the tongue is an unruly evil that is full of deadly poison. Strong words! Paul warned us to bless and curse not (see Rom. 12:14). When we curse anything, we speak ill of it. Think about it for a minute. When Jesus cursed the fig tree, it withered from the roots up (see Mark 11:12-25). Studies show that when we talk to plants, they react. If you say nice things to plants, they thrive. If you curse the plants, they suffer.

Interestingly, Jezebel cursed Elijah with a death threat—but she also cursed herself, vowing, "So may the gods do to me and more so, if by about this time tomorrow I do not make your life like the life of one of them" (1 Kings 19:2 NASB). Elijah felt the effects of the witchcraft, but the curse did not prevail against him. It backfired on Jezebel. Jezebel ended up dead when Jehu told the eunuchs to throw her down from her high tower. The dogs licked up her blood. The curse was reversed and Jezebel was no more.

We see a similar phenomenon with David and Goliath. Goliath cursed David by his gods saying, "Come to me, and I will give your flesh to the birds of the air and the beasts of the field!" (1 Sam. 17:44) David understood his covenant and didn't let the curse get in his head. He reversed the curse in Goliath's hearing in 1 Samuel 17:45-47:

> *You come to me with a sword, with a spear, and with a javelin. But I come to you in the name of the Lord of hosts, the God of the armies of Israel, whom you have defied. This day the Lord will deliver you into my hand, and I will strike you and take your head from you. And this day I will give the carcasses of the camp of the Philistines to the birds of the air and the wild beasts of the earth, that all the earth may know that there is a God in Israel. Then all this assembly shall know that the Lord does not save with sword and spear; for the battle is the Lord's, and He will give you into our hands.*

And so it was.

## BREAKING EVIL PROPHETIC DECREES

As I wrote in my book *Decrees That Make the Devil Flee*, much like a curse an evil decree is wicked, fleshly, and demonic. Evil decrees aim to cause you harm, misfortune, suffering, sorrow, distress, or calamity. Although there are some similarities, an evil decree is beyond a word curse. That's why I started adding the revocation and breaking of evil decrees to my daily prayer.

Again, a decree is more than a confession. A decree is an order that carries the force of law. A decree is a command or an ordinance. A decree is similar to a curse. A curse is a "prayer or invocation for harm or injury to come upon one." Goliath cursed David by his gods, but David decreed his victory. Curses must be broken. Evil decrees must also be broken and reversed.

God's decrees are just and righteous. God's decrees lead to life and health. God's decrees lead us into His purposes and prosperity. Evil decrees, also called demonic decrees, work the enemy's plans and purposes in our life. God's decrees are congruent with His nature to give us life in abundance, to the full, until it overflows. Evil decrees are congruent with the enemy's nature to steal, kill, and destroy. Evil decrees release evil spirits to enforce the enemy's will in your life.

## EVIL DECREES IN THE BIBLE

We see evil decrees throughout the pages of the Bible. Pharaoh's decree that all male Israelite babies be drowned in the water was over fear of losing power: "Pharaoh charged all his people, saying,

'You must cast every son that is born into the river, and you must preserve every daughter's life'" (Exod. 1:22 MEV).

This was a mass slaughter. There were 600,000 Israelite men in Egypt, which would lead me to believe there were at least 600,000 Israelite women and hundreds of thousands of babies sacrificed to Leviathan in the Nile River during Pharaoh's reign.

Could there be an evil decree over you that's causing what you birth in your life to be devoured by the enemy? Businesses have failed because of evil decrees. Dreams have been destroyed because of evil decrees. Relationships have failed. Finances have collapsed. Health has been destroyed. Minds have been tormented. But you can break and reverse these evil decrees, in the name of Jesus!

## KING NEBUCHADNEZZAR'S EVIL DECREE

King Nebuchadnezzar issued a decree that led Shadrach, Meshach, and Abednego into the fiery furnace because people were jealous. We read the account in Daniel 3:8-18 (MEV):

> *Therefore at that time certain Chaldeans came near and accused the Jews. They spoke and said to King Nebuchadnezzar, "O king, live forever. You, O king, have made a decree, that every man who hears the sound of the cornet, flute, harp, sackbut, psaltery, and dulcimer, and all kinds of music should fall down and worship the golden image. And whoever does not fall down and worship should be cast into the midst of a burning fiery furnace. There are certain Jews whom*

*you have set over the affairs of the province of Babylon: Shadrach, Meshach, and Abednego. These men, O king, have not regarded you. They do not serve your gods or worship the golden image which you have set up."*

*Then Nebuchadnezzar in his rage and fury commanded Shadrach, Meshach, and Abednego be brought. Then they brought these men before the king. Nebuchadnezzar spoke and said to them, "Is it true, Shadrach, Meshach, and Abednego, that you do not serve my gods or worship the golden image which I have set up? Now if you are ready at the time you hear the sound of the cornet, flute, harp, sackbut, psaltery, and dulcimer, and all kinds of music to fall down and worship the image which I have made, very well. But if you do not worship, you shall be cast the same hour into the midst of a burning fiery furnace. And who is that god who can deliver you out of my hands?"*

*Shadrach, Meshach, and Abednego answered and said to the king, "O Nebuchadnezzar, we do not need to give you an answer in this matter. If it be so, our God whom we serve is able to deliver us from the burning fiery furnace, and He will deliver us out of your hand, O king. But even if He does not, be it known to you, O king, that we will not serve your gods, nor worship the golden image which you have set up."*

You know the rest of the story. These three men of God ended up in a fiery furnace that was turned up to seven times the typical temperature. Thank God for deliverance from evil decrees!

## REVERSING EVIL DECREES

An evil decree can be broken and reversed through a higher decree. God is not pleased with the evil decrees we release over ourselves or the evil decrees jealous, offended, and otherwise wicked people release over us by inspiration of the enemy.

Take heart in Isaiah 49:24-27 (MEV):

> *Can the prey be taken from the mighty or the captives of a tyrant be delivered? For thus says the Lord: Even the captives of the mighty shall be taken away, and the prey of the tyrant shall be delivered; for I will contend with him who contends with you, and I will save your sons. I will feed those who oppress you with their own flesh, and they shall be drunk with their own blood as with sweet wine. And all flesh shall know that I, the Lord, am your Savior and your Redeemer, the Mighty One of Jacob.*

Please remember this: we're not wrestling against flesh and blood alone. The enemy inspires people to release evil decrees. So when we break and reverse evil decrees, we are not seeking to harm those the enemy used against us. We're essentially sending the evil back into the enemy's camp so we can walk in God's blessing.

When we love God, He will fight for us and, as our king and judge, will turn the evil decree back on the enemy when we trust Him and take authority over the wicked words, indictments, and judgments against us.

## A PRAYER TO BREAK EVIL DECREES

You can use this prayer as a model:

> *I come against every decree spoken over my life, my family, my finances, my health, my relationships, and my destiny, in Jesus' name. I plead the blood of Jesus, which speaks of better things. I take authority over all the power of the enemy, including every word curse, hex, vex, spell, incantation, and potion, in the name of Jesus. I decree the blessing and favor of God over every area of my life. I say I am blessed, peaceful, joyful, and prosperous. I walk in divine health. My spirit, soul, and body are whole, in Jesus' name.*

# CHAPTER 6

# DELIVERANCE FROM
# FINANCIAL
# WITCHCRAFT

Shortly after I was saved, I went to a Pentecostal church full of fire. The praise and worship was explosive, and people were coming from all over to get delivered from the demonic ties that bound them. The preaching was relevant and got you up on your feet. I was there every time the doors were open. That is, until I discerned a false prophet in the house.

The visiting minister was from the Caribbean Islands. I do not remember a word he preached, but I do remember the altar call. He called up all the entrepreneurs to receive a blessing from God. I was an entrepreneur—a freelance journalist—so I responded to the altar call. There were not many of us, but we all waited in expectant faith for the blessing.

Instead of praying for us, though, he pulled out handkerchiefs with hundred-dollar bills printed on them. He was reciting something about how handkerchiefs that had touched Paul's body carried miracle-working power. I didn't know anything about that since I was just saved. Later, I would find out that what he was saying was true, but he was taking the truth out of context. He was essentially twisting Scripture for his greedy gain.

The false prophet proceeded to tell those of us in the prayer line that when we sowed $100 he would give us one of these handkerchiefs and everything we put our hand to would automatically prosper. Again, he was twisting Scripture. Everything we put our hand to does prosper as we are obedient to the Lord, not because of some special handkerchief (see Deut. 30:9). I didn't know that Scripture, either, but something felt off. My spirit wasn't bearing witness to that word. I didn't know it at the time, but it was financial witchcraft.

Eagerly, everybody in the prayer line worked to scrounge up $100. This was a church of humble and relatively poor people. They didn't have it to give, but they were convinced if they believed the prophet they would prosper (see 2 Chron. 20:20). This was perhaps the height of prophetic manipulation. These poor souls were paying $100 for a handkerchief you could buy for ninety-nine cents at Walmart. The handkerchief did not have any special power, other than a false sign that helped entice people to give to the false prophet.

I was just a few weeks old in the Lord, but I discerned by the Holy Spirit within me that this man was a fraud. I was disappointed and somewhat disillusioned. I am grateful that the Lord did not allow me to become bitter against the prophetic because of this experience. Many do. I still wonder how many of those precious people figured out they had been deceived. The magic handkerchief was only good for wiping the tears away from their eyes when they saw they had wasted $100 they couldn't afford to lose.

Have you ever wondered what happens when you sow into a false prophet? Do you get a return on that investment? Or is it lost for good? How does God feel about you sowing Kingdom seed into the dark kingdom from which He delivered you? What do you do if you've discovered you are the victim of financial witchcraft? Can God restore what the enemy stole in your ignorance?

## GOD WARNS US OF FINANCIAL WITCHCRAFT

First, let's look at the reality of how God warns us of these shysters. He would not warn us over and over again about prophets and financial witchcraft if this were not a serious and age-old problem. These practices were employed in the days of Ezekiel and Jeremiah. They were deployed in the days of Peter and John. And they are ramping up.

Charles Spurgeon, an English preacher from the 1900s whose writings remain influential into the 21$^{st}$ century, once prophesied, "A time will come when instead of shepherds feeding the sheep, the church will have clowns entertaining the goats!" We're in those times, and, again, it's going to get worse. The Internet age makes it possible to scam people at the speed of light through social media.

Let's look at a few of God's warnings. Ezekiel prophesied, "'In you they take bribes to shed blood; you take usury and increase; you have made profit from your neighbors by extortion, and have forgotten Me,' says the Lord God" (Ezek. 22:12). Jeremiah prophesied, "Because from the least of them even to the greatest of them, everyone is given to covetousness; and from the prophet even to the priest, everyone deals falsely" (Jer. 6:13).

Peter also offered warnings: "By covetousness they will exploit you with deceptive words; for a long time their judgment has not been idle, and their destruction does not slumber" (2 Pet. 2:3). And again, "Having eyes full of adultery and that cannot cease from sin, enticing unstable souls. They have a heart trained in covetous practices, and are accursed children" (2 Pet. 2:14).

We really can't say we weren't warned, yet we still fall for prophetic money scams. The so-called Nigerian prince scam is quite obvious. Here's how it works: you get an email from someone offering you a large sum of money, but you have to give them a payment to transfer the money. Usually it's connected to an inheritance from someone who died—a long lost relative of yours or someone who just wants to bless you. People still fall for this, which is why propagators keep broadcasting these emails.

Then there's the orphanage scam. People contact you on social media pretending to be someone else. I can't tell you how many of my followers have sown into an orphanage after being prophesied to in my name, though clearly my name was not spelled correctly and I do not pimp for money. Then there are deliverance ministers who insist if you sowed large sums of money into witchcraft you have to give even larger seeds to God to secure and seal your deliverance. This is heresy!

## PROPHETIC MONEY SCAMS ABOUND

There's no lack of prophetic money scams. Unfortunately, some-times these horror stories appear in secular media, which brings true prophets under scrutiny. Don't get me wrong. I am glad it's being exposed. But it paints all prophets with the same brush. According to News24, a woman in Namibia found herself homeless after a false pastor manipulated her into selling her house to pay for his prayers.

"While relating her story, the victim claimed that Shinima told her that her house was possessed by demons and that something bad would happen to her if she did not sell the property off imme-diately," News24 reports.[1] "After selling her house for R1.4m, the woman is said to have withdrawn R980,000 to give to the alleged holy man, who then only gave her R15,000 to cover her expenses going forward." Following the exchange, the victim alleged that Shinima disappeared, switching off his phone and moving away from his "church."

A woman in South Africa spent more than half a million rand to get rid of recurring headaches and find love. A false prophet left her almost R600,000 in debt and struggling worse than she was before, according to News24.

"During the consultation he told me about my life and every-thing he said was true. He told me I had recently separated from my husband and I had a spiritual husband who was always walking with me," the woman said. "He told me I often see a shadow of a person and that I felt someone was with me even when I'm alone. He said I had problems at work because they favoured a new employee over me even though she does not know the work. He even told me about my headaches."[2]

Those may seem like extreme examples that you wouldn't fall for. But many people do get taken in by such scams because they are hungry for direction in their lives. They are so desperate, it seems, they forget that God would willingly pour out His wisdom liberally if they would just seek His face earnestly. I personally received an email from a "Master Prophet," though I have no idea how I got on this list. The email was wrought with financial witchcraft. It read:

---

Act now! Watch your future come alive now! God is transforming you completely. This will make you confident, full of belief and satisfied about the outcome to your situation.

1. A prophet will call you and speak with you one-on-one.

2. A prophetic word for your relief will be in their mouth for you.

3. This word of prophecy will be recorded for you to hear again.

4. I will email this important prophetic word to you.

5. I will prophesy on an MP3 or CD all about your life.

6. I will ask another prophet to join me, and together we will prophesy about you.

Of course, the instructions are to send money first. None of this is new. People have sold miracle water, miracle sawdust, and pumped obedience offerings, declaring, "God just spoke to me that if you will obey God with a double portion prove God offering of $38 by faith, we can claim a thousand-fold return."

I am not a fan of preachers who suggest we should give certain amounts. I'm not saying God can't suggest specific amounts, but some preachers seem to have a number—and often a big number—in mind for every offering. But Paul's Spirit-inspired words tell us we should give according to what we've decided in our heart (see 2 Cor. 9:7).

I was in a meeting with a Christian TV minister with a household name—if I called his name you would know him—who came to a church I was attending at the time for one night only. There must have been 1,000 of us in the sanctuary. He was pressuring people for over thirty minutes to sow a one-thousand dollar seed. Many people did. I was shocked at the pressure. Others ministers have used the "sow $638" and you'll tap into Luke 6:38, "Give, and it will be given to you: good measure, pressed down, shaken together, and running over will be put into your bosom."

Then there's the thousand-fold return promise offering, based on Deuteronomy 1:11, "May the Lord God of your fathers make you a thousand times more numerous than you are, and bless you as He has promised you!" Usually, these types of ministries have portable credit card machines so you can sow immediately—before you change your mind. Again, I'm not saying people should not be challenged to stretch in their giving. Much of the church gives very little and most Christians don't tithe. But our pleas should be based on God's pure Word, not twisted Scripture promising something God never said.

## WHAT HAPPENS TO YOUR SEED?

So what happens when you sow into a false prophet? Do you get a return on that investment? I don't believe so. There are different kinds of soils. If you sow in bad soil, the seed cannot grow. Think about it in the natural. Most crops do poorly in bad soil. Degraded soil makes farms less fertile and threatens food supplies. From a spiritual perspective, consider the Parable of the Sower in Matthew 13:1-9:

> *On the same day Jesus went out of the house and sat by the sea. And great multitudes were gathered together to Him, so that He got into a boat and sat; and the whole multitude stood on the shore.*
>
> *Then He spoke many things to them in parables, saying: "Behold, a sower went out to sow. And as he sowed, some seed fell by the wayside; and the birds came and devoured them. Some fell on stony places, where they did not have much earth; and they immediately sprang up because they had no depth of earth. But when the sun was up they were scorched, and because they had no root they withered away. And some fell among thorns, and the thorns sprang up and choked them. But others fell on good ground and yielded a crop: some a hundredfold, some sixty, some thirty. He who has ears to hear, let him hear!"*

Think of the seed you sow into false prophets as seed that falls by the wayside. The false prophets—the birds—come and devour it. You are not sowing into the Kingdom of God. You are sowing into the kingdom of darkness. Spurgeon once said, "When that which comes of his sowing is unfruitful, the sower's work is wasted: he has spent his strength for nothing. Without fruit the sower's work would even seem to be insane, for he takes good wheat, throws it away, and loses it in the ground."[3]

Manipulated by financial witchcraft, people who sow into false prophets don't see the promised breakthrough. They don't see the thousand-fold return. They don't see the new car, the new house, or the right spouse. They don't see anything but an empty pocketbook. What's happening? Haggai 1:6 (AMPC) is in effect:

> You have sown much, but you have reaped little; you eat, but you do not have enough; you drink, but you do not have your fill; you clothe yourselves, but no one is warm; and he who earns wages has earned them to put them in a bag with holes in it.

The verse before that is clear, "Consider your ways" (Hag. 1:5). God wants us to use our seed to build His house, not the house of false prophets.

Repeatedly, Scripture shows us it's possible to sow seed to no effect. Deuteronomy 28:38 (CSB) reveals, "You will sow much seed in the field but harvest little, because locusts will devour it." Isaiah 5:10 (NET) tells us, "Indeed, a large vineyard will produce just a few gallons, and enough seed to yield several bushels will produce less than a bushel."

Then there's Jeremiah 12:13 (CSB), which reads, "They have sown wheat but harvested thorns. They have exhausted themselves but have no profit. Be put to shame by your harvests because of the Lord's burning anger." Hosea 8:7 (CSB) says, "Indeed, they sow the wind and reap the whirlwind. There is no standing grain; what sprouts fails to yield flour. Even if they did, foreigners would swallow it up."

When we sow into the wrong soil, or when we sow with the wrong motive or into the wrong kingdom, we don't get what we expect. Our hope was invested in the wrong field. God promises to rebuke the devourer and pour out a blessing you can't contain when you bring your tithes and offerings into the storehouse, not the false prophet's house.

## WE NEED TO REPENT

Before you feel sorry for yourself or get bitter, understand this is not just affecting you. When you sow into the ministry of a false prophet or teacher, you are funding their evil work. And it's not all about money. It's the time you sow into their ministry. It's the social media shares and likes you give them, sharing their deception with innocent people who rely on your integrity to discern before you hit the share button. God is not mad at you, but you do have the responsibility to be a good steward and to discern these things and avoid them. Paul wrote:

> *But now I have written to you not to keep company with anyone named a brother, who is sexually immoral, or covetous, or an idolater, or a reviler, or a drunkard, or an extortioner—not even to eat with such a person. For*

*what have I to do with judging those also who are out-
side? Do you not judge those who are inside? But those
who are outside God judges. Therefore "put away from
yourselves the evil person"* (1 Corinthians 5:11-13).

I've seen deceived people defend false prophets and teachers not
just to the bitter end—but to their bitter end. They are deceiving
and being deceived. We don't want to call that which is evil good,
so we need to repent. Ask God to forgive you if you have sown into
a false ministry or served as a propaganda machine for false ministries. You didn't realize it at the time. You were ignorant of the
devil's devices. But now God has opened your eyes. Thank Him and
repent. And be part of the solution.

## GOD WILL WORK IT FOR GOOD

Many people when they realize they've been scammed feel stupid,
guilty, ashamed, or even condemned. That's not the right response.
Anyone can be deceived. Be grateful that God delivered you from
financial witchcraft, and when the enemy works to condemn you,
remind him of Romans 8:1, "There is therefore now no condemnation to those who are in Christ Jesus, who do not walk according to
the flesh, but according to the Spirit."

What's more, remind him—and yourself—of Romans 8:28,
"And we know that all things work together for good to those who
love God, to those who are the called according to His purpose."
*The Message* translation of that verse reads, "That's why we can be

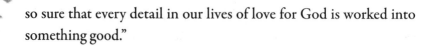

so sure that every detail in our lives of love for God is worked into something good."

And The Passion Translation offers, "So we are convinced that every detail of our lives is continually woven together to fit into God's perfect plan of bringing good into our lives, for we are his lovers who have been called to fulfill his designed purpose." What good will He work from it? It was an expensive lesson. Maybe you will discern it next time. You can warn others. And God can restore what the enemy stole.

## WHAT HAPPENS TO THE FALSE PROPHET?

You might wonder, what happens to that false prophet or false teacher—or false pastor—who stole my money? It's a good question. We need to pray that they will also repent before it's too late because it won't go well for them if they continue robbing God in the name of Jesus. Exodus 20:15 makes it plain, "You shall not steal." False prophets aren't holding you up at gunpoint, but they are wearing masks of manipulation and bending your will with financial witchcraft.

Jesus was clear, "No one can serve two masters; for either he will hate the one and love the other, or else he will be loyal to the one and despise the other. You cannot serve God and mammon" (Matt. 6:24). Make no mistake, false prophets are not serving God. They are serving other gods, usually Jezebel, Baal, and Mammon. False prophets fit the bill of Psalm 10:3, "For the wicked boasts of his heart's desire; he blesses the greedy *and* renounces the Lord."

If money is your motive for doing ministry, you've already missed it and you've already grieved the Holy Spirit. Deception can't be too far off. Paul warned his spiritual son Timothy about money-motivated ministry: "For the love of money is a root of all kinds of evil, for which some have strayed from the faith in their greediness, and pierced themselves through with many sorrows" (1 Tim. 6:10).

Many times you see the lives of false prophets falling apart behind the scenes. Their marriages end in divorce or their health fails. This is the fulfillment of Proverbs 15:27, "He who is greedy for gain troubles his own house." Proverbs 28:20 tells us, "He who hastens to be rich will not go unpunished." Proverbs 22:16-17 says the one who oppresses the poor "will surely come to poverty."

Isaiah prophesied, "For the iniquity of his covetousness I was angry and struck him; I hid and was angry, and he went on backsliding in the way of his heart" (Isa. 57:17). That's intense, and so is Jeremiah 8:10, "Therefore I will give their wives to others, and their fields to those who will inherit them; because from the least even to the greatest everyone is given to covetousness; from the prophet even to the priest everyone deals falsely."

Paul made it clear thieves and covetous people and extortioners will not inherit the Kingdom of God (see 1 Cor. 6:10). And Peter has a warning for pastors:

> *Shepherd the flock of God which is among you, serving as overseers, not by compulsion but willingly, not for dishonest gain but eagerly; nor as being lords over those entrusted to you, but being examples to the flock* (1 Peter 5:2-3).

With all that in mind, consider Jeremiah 5:26-29 the icing on the false prophet's cake:

> *"For among My people are found wicked men; they lie in wait as one who sets snares; they set a trap; they catch men. As a cage is full of birds, so their houses are full of deceit. Therefore they have become great and grown rich. They have grown fat, they are sleek; yes, they surpass the deeds of the wicked; they do not plead the cause, the cause of the fatherless; yet they prosper, and the right of the needy they do not defend. Shall I not punish them for these things?" says the Lord.*

We do need to pray for false ones to repent. Anyone can be restored up to a point. There comes a time when a person has rejected Holy Spirit's conviction and their conscience is seared with a hot iron (see 1 Tim. 4:2). God can give them over to a reprobate mind (see Rom. 1:28), and they are trapped in a strong delusion (see 2 Thess. 2:11).

So we pray they will repent like Zacchaeus the tax collector who extorted money from Israelites. We pray they will walk in Ezekiel 33:15, "If the wicked restores the pledge, gives back what he has stolen, and walks in the statutes of life without committing iniquity, he shall surely live; he shall not die."

## RECOVERING FROM FINANCIAL WITCHCRAFT

So how do you recover if you've been hoodwinked by a purveyor of financial witchcraft? Proverbs 10:22 says the blessing of the Lord makes you rich without sorrow. Matthew 6:33 admonishes us to seek first the Kingdom of God and His righteousness and everything else we need will be given to us.

The first thing you need to do is start tithing to a healthy ministry. Until you get your finances back in Kingdom order, you won't see restoration. Next, respect money. Never spend it before you have it or you are borrowing against your future at a high rate of interest.

You can't expect God to give you money if you don't respect money. Everything belongs to God, including any money you worked for. He owns the cattle on a thousand hills—and He owns the hills on which the cattle graze (see Ps. 50:10). The silver is His and the gold is His (see Hag. 2:8). Don't waste what God has put in your hand. Don't abuse money. Christian personal finance expert Dave Ramsey once said, "You must gain control over your money or the lack of it will forever control you."

Develop a discipline with the money you do have. Do you really need that new car? Do you really need to go to the nail salon? Do you really need that new purse? Do you really need to go out to lunch and coffee every day? Studies show millionaires are usually frugal. Create a budget and stick to it. Stop charging everything on your credit cards. Pay them down instead.

Finding financial independence requires a lot of little efforts that eventually add up. At first, it will seem like you aren't making any progress. You have to be disciplined and persistent. If you stick with it long enough, you will see it working. Your efforts will begin to bear fruit. You will begin to pull ahead. Your finances will improve and your debts will disappear. Your bank account will grow and your whole life will improve.

The bottom line is we need to be good stewards of what God gives us. Jesus said, "He who is faithful in what is least is faithful also in much; and he who is unjust in what is least is unjust also in much. Therefore if you have not been faithful in the unrighteous mammon, who will commit to your trust the true riches?" (Luke 16:10-11).

## NOTES

1. News24, "Namibian 'pastor' tricks woman into selling house in exchange for prayers," June 27, 2016, https://www.news24 .com/News24/namibian-pastor-tricks-woman-into-selling -house-in-exchange-for-prayers-20160627; accessed March 22, 2023.

2. Thembisile Makgalemele, "'I was scammed out of R600k by fake prophet,' says woman alone and broke after being duped," April 20, 2018, https://www.snl24.com/drum/news/i-was -scammed-out-of-r600-000-by-a-fake-prophet-20180420; accessed March 22, 2023.

3. Charles Spurgeon, "Sown Among Thorns," August 19, 1888, Metropolitan Tabernacle, Newington.

# CHAPTER 7

# DELIVERANCE FROM
# RELATIONAL
# WITCHCRAFT

I f you leave, I'll kill myself." Those were the words of a desperate abuser who had gotten away with murdering his wife's confidence for years. Cal was a drunk and had a history of abuse, but Sandy had already been married four times before and kept falling into the same trap. It's a trap I call relational witchcraft.

Sandy was stuck in a toxic cycle, knowing she should leave her abusive husband but afraid to walk out the door for fear he would follow through on his suicide threats. She had pre-guilt. He hadn't done anything and wasn't planning to, but the pre-guilt of him shooting himself in the head haunted her.

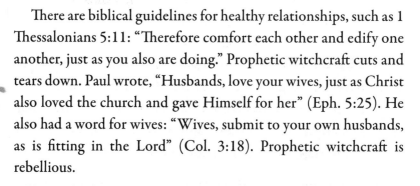

Sandy would leave temporarily but kept going back to Cal over and over again because of a toxic soul tie and the repetitive cycle of feeling like she could fix the men she loved. Sandy finally left Cal because she was literally afraid he would kill her. Put another way, she was more fearful for her safety than she was of his suicide. It took years for Sandy to break free from the emotional bondage that continued to trap her in this relational witchcraft cycle.

Of course, this is an extreme example of relational witchcraft—so extreme that if you don't know the signs of relationship witchcraft, you might not believe you're stuck in this type of relationship. Domestic violence—or the threat of domestic violence—isn't always present with relational witchcraft. Emotional and psychological abuse is sometimes more subtle. And it's not always a romantic relationship. Relational witchcraft can manifest between friends, employees and employers, and family members.

There are biblical guidelines for healthy relationships, such as 1 Thessalonians 5:11: "Therefore comfort each other and edify one another, just as you also are doing." Prophetic witchcraft cuts and tears down. Paul wrote, "Husbands, love your wives, just as Christ also loved the church and gave Himself for her" (Eph. 5:25). He also had a word for wives: "Wives, submit to your own husbands, as is fitting in the Lord" (Col. 3:18). Prophetic witchcraft is rebellious.

Prophetic witchcraft is selfish and self-centered. Solomon wrote, "A friend loves at all times, and a brother is born for adversity" (Prov. 17:17). Prophetic witchcraft loves conditionally and brings adversity into your life. Paul encourages us to walk "with all lowliness and gentleness, with longsuffering, bearing with one another in love, endeavoring to keep the unity of the Spirit in the bond of peace" (Eph. 4:2-3). You get the idea. So how do you know if you've experienced relational witchcraft?

## WHAT IS RELATIONAL WITCHCRAFT?

If you are in bondage to relational witchcraft, you may know it—or you may not. Unfortunately, this type of abuse comes with so much shame that people don't want to expose it—or even believe this is what's really happening to them. But there are clear signs.

Let me first define relational witchcraft. Relational witchcraft can involve prophetic witchcraft, but it can also be a work of the flesh. Witchcraft as a work of the flesh is listed in Galatians 5:19-21:

> *Now the works of the flesh are evident, which are: adultery, fornication, uncleanness, lewdness, idolatry, sorcery, hatred, contentions, jealousies, outbursts of wrath, selfish ambitions, dissensions, heresies, envy, murders, drunkenness, revelries, and the like; of which I tell you beforehand, just as I also told you in time past, that those who practice such things will not inherit the kingdom of God.*

Many of the works of the flesh mark relational witchcraft, even beyond witchcraft itself (or what the New King James Version calls "sorcery"). The Greek word for *witchcraft* in the context of a fleshly work is *pharmakeia*. It means, "poisoning, sorcery, magical arts found in connection with idolatry and fostered by it," according to *The KJV New Testament Greek Lexicon*. The lexicon even offers a metaphor: the deceptions and seductions of idolatry. People operating in relational witchcraft, which may or may not have a prophetic element, essentially idolize themselves.

I've seen this in the family dynamic. We call these toxic relationships. Maybe it's a controlling mother who doesn't know how to respect your boundaries. Or maybe it's an elder sibling who wants to call the shots. A woman in our church, we'll call her Theresa, found herself in bondage to relational witchcraft. After a divorce, she moved back home and moved in with her father. Her father was operating in textbook relational witchcraft with harsh demands that never ended. Meanwhile, her brother was trying to control her spiritual life. She was hemmed in on all sides and afraid to make a move without approval from the family for fear of the backlash.

Finally, her brother was caught red-handed operating in prophetic witchcraft one too many times in our church community. This behavior was corrected, and corrected again and again over several years, but suddenly the spirit influencing him went into overdrive. This man had been secretly luring women in the church to himself and pulling out of them intimate details of their struggles to create soul ties he could use to control them. When the depth of this deception was exposed, our team of elders immediately confronted the man and asked him to leave the church. He didn't even try to repent.

Of course, we knew all proverbial hell was about to break loose. We called Theresa in and exposed enough of the drama to confirm what she already knew about her brother. Theresa had a choice: she could either leave our church, where she was growing by leaps and bounds, or she could stand up to her misguided brother and keep coming. We knew the church was going to see massive retaliation in the spirit over this showdown, but we also knew Theresa would get the brunt of the warfare if she didn't follow her brother out the door. Theresa prayed and stayed. Meanwhile, reports are the brother is now in another church repeating the same behaviors.

So what are some signs? I'm going to share a slew of thoughts below. Keep in mind, you don't have to be experiencing all these signs to mark someone's behavior—or your feelings as a result of their behavior—as relational witchcraft. Also keep in mind that everyone has bad days. You're not going on a witch hunt here. You are looking for eye-opening patterns based on one or more of these behaviors that repeats itself over time and causes damage to your soul.

## SIGNS OF RELATIONAL WITCHCRAFT

When you are the victim of relational witchcraft, you constantly feel drained. That's because relational witchcraft is laced with drama. Where there is relational witchcraft, there is constant drama. You don't or can't truly trust someone operating in relational witchcraft because they will use personal, private information against you. They will talk about you behind your back or even stab you in the back. You are walking on eggshells much of the time and never know when the conversation is going to turn sour or verbally violent.

Again, you are dealing with constant drama. People operating in relational witchcraft expect you to take on their offenses. Know this: 1 Thessalonians 4:11 tells us we should "aspire to lead a quiet life, to mind your own business." People operating in relational witchcraft also typically operate in gossip, slander, and strife, which leads to confusion and evil every work (see Jam. 3:16). When someone in your life has drama with everyone else they know, consider this: they are the common denominator.

People operating in relational witchcraft often lie. When you catch them in a lie, they will refuse to acknowledge it. Lying is an abomination to the Lord (see Prov. 12:22). A person "who breathes out lies will perish" (Prov. 19:9 ESV). Paul warned Christians, "Do not lie to one another, since you have put off the old man with his deeds" (Col. 3:9). You may feel like you are constantly in a toxic game as they stonewall and gaslight you based on their lies and manipulation.

Beyond this, if you are in relationship with someone operating in witchcraft you may find yourself constantly criticized, condemned, guilted, or ignored. Your accuser or abuser will always find something wrong with you. They nitpick. Nothing is ever good enough. They set themselves up as your judge, despite Jesus' warning in Matthew 7:1: "Judge not, that you be not judged." They stand in their own sin casting stones at you. They are putting a stumbling block in your path, raging against Paul's warning in Romans 14:13, "Therefore let us not judge one another anymore, but rather resolve this, not to put a stumbling block or a cause to fall in our brother's way."

If you're embroiled in relational witchcraft, you may find yourself being threatened or abused or just cower under the incessant intimidation tactics—whether financial, emotional, mental, or spiritual—that work to keep you under their thumb. Peter tells us plainly, "And who is he who will harm you if you become followers of what is good? But even if you should suffer for righteousness' sake, you are blessed. 'And do not be afraid of their threats, nor be troubled'" (1 Pet. 3:13-14).

People operating in relational witchcraft bring out the worst in you. Paul put it this way: "Do not be deceived: 'Evil company corrupts good habits'" (1 Cor. 15:33). Solomon wrote, "Make no friendship with an angry man, and with a furious man do not go, lest you learn his ways and set a snare for your soul" (Prov. 22:24-25). You feel unsupported. You can't be true to yourself. You are being held back. You may become an emotional wreck.

The more entangled you get with someone operating in relational witchcraft, the more trapped you feel. You can't be honest about your emotions without risking backlash. Your needs in the relationship don't matter. Your friends or family are telling you the relationship is sour or perverted, but you can't bring yourself to believe it. You are miserable. You live stressed or depressed. You are insecure. But you think you can somehow change the pattern. In this case, relational witchcraft has deceived you.

Love should mark our relationships because God is love. Paul wrote this revelatory reminder in 1 Corinthians 13:4-7:

> *Love suffers long and is kind; love does not envy; love does not parade itself, is not puffed up; does not behave rudely, does not seek its own, is not provoked, thinks no evil; does not rejoice in iniquity, but rejoices in the truth; bears all things, believes all things, hopes all things, endures all things.*

No relationship is perfect, but if love is not the prevailing spirit something is wrong. We cite Paul's words in 2 Corinthians 6:14 about not being unequally yoked with unbelievers. That's a relevant truth, but here's another one: you can also be unequally yoked with believers. Someone can be a Christian and have serious emotional issues—or even demons—that drive them to control and manipulate you. It's up to you to take a stand against relational witchcraft. Proverbs 13:20 tells us the companion of fools will suffer harm.

## WHY IT'S SO HARD TO LEAVE

I've never witnessed anyone have an easy time breaking free from relational witchcraft. It seems hard to leave someone even when you see it. And after you leave, despite the freedom, there always seems to be a period of second-guessing yourself. Was it really all that bad? Did God want you to stay and pray for them and help them break free? The mind battle is real. Beyond that, there are many other reasons why it can be seem difficult or impossible to leave.

Sandy's toxic cycle went on for years. She would get the courage to tell her husband she was leaving and he would pull out the crocodile tears and threaten to kill himself. As mentioned, a few times she did leave but went back in the face of his threats. She said she would feel terrible if he committed suicide because she left.

Of course, he knew that and because the threat kept working he kept issuing it. This reminds me of Proverbs 26:11, "As a dog returns to his own vomit, so a fool repeats his folly." Returning to an abuser is foolish. This was a toxic cycle that repeated itself until she finally got the courage to buy a plane ticket and fly to another city for refuge. He did not kill himself. Sandy's issue here was a soul tie, which we talked about in another chapter.

There are other reasons why people don't escape relational witchcraft. A few of them are the time investment you've made, codependency, and fear of retaliation. When you've invested your life—and your heart—into a person or organization, it can be difficult to up and leave. You feel somewhat responsible for them. You don't want to think you've wasted your time. It can be daunting to start all over again in a new relationship. Sometimes, there are even financial ties or children to consider. Then there's the shame of a broken relationship. But remember, Jesus bore all your shame when He hung on a cross (see Heb. 12:2).

If a codependency has formed, it can make it difficult to break away from the relationship. Codependency is sort of like a soul tie, but different. Codependency marks a relationship in which a person manifesting low self-esteem and a strong desire for approval has an unhealthy attachment to another often controlling or manipulative person, according to *Merriam-Webster*'s dictionary. Signs of codependency manifest as difficultly making decisions without the other person, difficulty communicating your feelings, people pleasing, lack of boundaries, the need to fix others, and being loyal to a fault. Remember Psalm 118:6, "The Lord is on my side; I will not fear. What can man do to me?"

## BREAKING FREE OF RELATIONAL WITCHCRAFT

The only way to stop relational witchcraft is to confront it. Sometimes—I might even say usually—that means ending the relationship. Yes, anyone can repent, but in the realm of relational witchcraft I've found the pattern continues unless the person has a radical encounter with God. Holding out hope they will repent when it's been months or years without any change and the Lord is leading you to sever ties is not wisdom. So how do you break free of relational witchcraft?

Reject denial. You may be in denial, which is the first stage of grief. Denial is a refusal to acknowledge the reality in which you find yourself. You may downplay how bad it is or how much you are hurt. You may avoid confronting how deep the wounds are because it's just too painful. If you are going to break free of relational witchcraft, discerning what's in you that needs to be healed is a must. This is more than healing from the last experience. This is determining the deeper root of the issue, especially if you keep finding yourself in abusive relationships.

Once you escape relational witchcraft, you'll need a support system that will encourage you not to go back. You'll need people around you with whom you can process the experience—people who will reassure you that you are not crazy. Once you catch your breath, you may start to grieve the good parts of the relationship. You may start to feel the pain of loss for what you had hoped the relationship would be but never could be. Here, again, you need that support system around you. Find those who will weep with you (see Rom. 12:15).

If you hope to heal and come out stronger, you'll need to forgive the person, not necessarily face to face or phone to phone but between you and God. Forgiveness is the first step to healing, but forgiveness doesn't always mean reconciliation. If you let the abuser back in your life without their deep repentance, they will continue to operate in witchcraft that convinces you that you are the problem. Cut the cord and break all connection, then forgive. Take the time to heal and to learn the lesson from the trial. If you don't learn the lesson, you may make the same mistake in your next relationship. Peter called this behavior like a sow pig that is washed and goes back to wallowing in the mud (see 2 Pet. 2:22). If God wants to restore the relationship, He will make that abundantly clear and the fruit of repentance will be obvious.

## DON'T LOOK BACK

Consider Paul the apostle's words in Philippians 3:13-14: "Brethren, I do not count myself to have apprehended; but one thing I do, forgetting those things which are behind and reaching forward to those things which are ahead, I press toward the goal for the prize of the upward call of God in Christ Jesus."

Forgetting those things which are behind so you can reach forward to those things which are ahead can bring gut-wrenching pain to your soul. I know that pain all too well as I have experienced it many times. To describe the process as difficult would be an understatement. Sometimes moving on feels like leaving a piece of yourself behind. Other times forgetting those things which are behind seems like an exercise in futility. Still other times reaching forward to those things which are ahead feels like a tug of war in your soul threatening to tear you apart.

Again, I know that pain all too well as I have experienced it many times. Forgetting those things which are behind is perhaps one of the greatest challenges we can face, especially when those "things" were a major part of our daily lives. I've had to "forget" a husband, more than one best friend, several ministries and more—and sometimes in the midst of great *persecution*. But I'm here to tell you that we can forget those things which are behind. Or at least we can remember them without the gut-wrenching pain we felt while we were making the transition. And we can press on toward the goal with joy.

## SOULISH REALITIES

It all starts in the mind. What we think about can live on as reality in our souls long after a painful event passes. I remember a difficult split with a friend who was emotionally unstable. This friend was dear to me on many levels, but not a week went by when she didn't have an emotional meltdown and attack me verbally for "not being a friend." She wanted from me what only Jesus could give her and was operating in relational witchcraft to manipulate me.

The *Holy Spirit* told me at one point to walk away if it happened again because it was abusive—and it was distracting me from God's will. And it wasn't helping her, either. But alas, soulish compassion can cloud spiritual discernment. It did indeed happen again, but I didn't obey God and walk away. Instead, I tried for another year to counsel her through her emotional issues with absolutely no fruit and subjected myself to witchcraft. In fact, it only got worse. I had become an enabler, of sorts. Finally, it got so bad that I had to cut the relationship out of my life altogether. And it was a painful cut for both of us.

Guilt, sadness, *condemnation*—a flood of emotions came to plague me. That's when I had to make a decision about what I was going to think about. The Bible says, "For as he thinks in his heart, so is he" (Prov. 23:7). The enemy wanted me to wallow in that guilt, sadness, and condemnation until I ran back to my friend with repentance and continued a relationship God had told me to cut off a year earlier.

## RESISTING THE PAST

I had to resist that temptation with everything in me at first. After all, everyone likes a familiar friend. And nobody likes to hurt a friend. I had to quickly grab hold of the reigns of my mind, stop replaying the scenes over and over again in my soul, and reach forward to those things which are ahead. The only way out is through, and it starts with a disciplined mind.

Maybe for you it's not a relationship, per se. Maybe you need to forget past hurts, past failures—or even past successes. The point is this: dwelling on an unpleasant past, no matter how recent or far away that past is, can't lead to healing. Dwelling on an unpleasant past isn't the path to *forgiveness*. Dwelling on an unpleasant past can't send you to the next place God wants to take you. It just can't. Dwelling on an unpleasant past can only keep you tied to that past, which hinders you from moving forward in God.

Beloved, if you were led by the *Spirit of God* to end your relationship with a person or place or if the enemy caused you to experience great loss in your life through death, divorce, or some other tragedy, God has something better for you. And if your past is one of shame, guilt, and condemnation for sins you've committed, God is ready, willing, and able to forgive you and cleanse you from all unrighteousness (see 1 John 1:9).

God is a progressive God. He's always moving forward. By His grace—and with a will determined not to dwell on an unpleasant past—we can overcome the challenge of forgetting those things that are behind. I won't lie to you. It won't be easy. The past may even come back to "haunt" you sometimes. But the battle really is in the mind. The good news is, you have the mind of Christ (see 1 Cor. 2:16) and God has a good plan for you. Press forward to that goal. Leave the past behind. Amen.

I heard the Lord say, "It's time to leave your past in the dust, shake the dust off your feet, and walk in the future and hope I have planned for you." Leaving your past in the dust often means renewing your mind. Look at Colossians 3:1-2 in *The Message*:

> *So if you're serious about living this new resurrection life with Christ, act like it. Pursue the things over which Christ presides. Don't shuffle along, eyes to the ground, absorbed with the things right in front of you. Look up, and be alert to what is going on around Christ—that's where the action is. See things from his perspective.*

What's Christ's perspective? His perspective is that we are overcomers. We are accepted in the beloved. We are not alone because He will never leave us or forsake us. We have the oil of joy, the garment of praise.

Let this be your confession:

> *Jesus, I am willing to press past my pain and into victory. I am more than a conqueror in You. You understand me. You know my hurts and my wounds and my grief and my loneliness. But You are here to deliver me. I refuse to remain in the past any longer. I exchange mourning for*

*joy, praise for heaviness. And I thank You, Lord, that I can press on toward the mark of the prize. Pain, you can't stay. I command you to leave my soul in the name of Jesus. I am free from pain. I am renewed in the spirit of my mind. I am victorious!*

# CHAPTER 8

# DELIVERANCE FROM WITCHCRAFT-INSPIRED SICKNESS AND DISEASE

One minute I was fine, the next minute I could barely move. I had black circles under my eyes. My body all but collapsed. I went from preaching on revival circuits to barely being about to get out of bed for more than a few hours a day.

The doctors could find nothing medically wrong with me. My bloodwork looked good. There was no real diagnosis, but my symptoms were oppressing. Some days were better than others. Sometimes I thought I was recovering only to have a setback. At one point, I even developed a stutter.

After about a year of this debilitating issue—after praying, warring, taking communion, renewing my mind—I starting to think this was going to be my new reality. I started to believe this was my lot in life. *Discouraged* is not a strong enough word for how I felt.

Despite all this, I kept persevering. I did as much as I could when I could. I maintained some speaking engagements and God's grace was sufficient, but afterward I would crash again. It was a mystery.

In January 2018, the Holy Spirit told me when I went to London I would be healed. But the London trip was six months away. It was a promise, but it seemed so far off. I felt like I was losing so many opportunities and so much momentum. It was miserable. When we traveled to Europe, we first stopped in Sweden. I was exhausted during that trip. Things seemed to get worse.

We flew to London and rested for a couple of days. I was still exhausted, and then it happened. On the last day of our journey, I woke up with a headache that was like no other headache I had ever experienced before or since. It wasn't a mere migraine, it was a spiritual attack of massive proportions. No amount of Excedrin or water or coffee even touched it. I was in so much pain at one point, I literally wanted to pull my hair out.

Suddenly, the pain left. In that moment, I got a phone call from the conference host saying there was a prophet in town who heard about this headache and he wanted to pray for me. I knew in my spirit this was the moment of deliverance from this spiritual attack. I knew I wasn't physically sick. Throughout the 18 months I suffered, I knew it was more spiritual than natural. I sort of felt like Job in those days.

I bounded down the stairs and met with this prophet. He started praying for me and saw in the spirit little ugly demons all around me. He began to break curses—many, many curses. Though not by name, his prophetic word even exposed who had released the curses. In that moment, it suddenly became completely obvious what had happened. I don't know why I couldn't break the attack myself, other than I couldn't see the source of it. Sometimes God sends someone to reveal what you can't see. And, as I always say, an enemy exposed is an enemy defeated. I got deliverance from the curse, and when I got home people told me I looked ten years younger. I really did!

## PROPHETIC WITCHCRAFT CAN MAKE YOU SICK

My story is dramatic. Your story may not be as dramatic. But make no mistake, prophetic witchcraft can bring infirmity into your household. When I was writing my first book on Jezebel, *The Spiritual Warrior's Guide to Defeating Jezebel*, I got sick six times in the course of a year. Yes, six times! I was hardly over one cold or flu before I got another cold or flu. This was especially unusual because I hadn't had as much as a sniffle in the five years before. Essentially, I was battling a cycle of infirmity—which, thank God, I finally overcame.

Then again when I started traveling to Europe every month to plant houses of prayer, I came home every single month sick for the first five months. I was fine while traveling through Europe, but would start manifesting sickness the moment I walked in the door at home. I was incapacitated for most of the next week, only to pick up and go again.

We broke the attack when we finally built up a thick enough prayer wall with intercessors to cover me on the journeys.

If you are sick all the time and the doctors find nothing wrong, it could be a demon afflicting you. You could be dealing with Jezebel's witchcraft. The Bible talks about Jezebel and her witchcrafts in 2 Kings 9:22. I believe infirmities are part of Jezebel's witchcrafts. Witchcraft is a spiritual force—one of the powers listed in Ephesians 6—that the enemy uses to attack us.

The word for *witchcraft* in 2 Kings 9:22 comes from the Hebrew *kesheph*. It means sorcery and witchcraft. *Merriam-Webster's* dictionary defines witchcraft as "the use of sorcery or magic, communication with a familiar." *Sorcery* is defined as "the use of magical powers that are obtained through evil spirits." The Queen Jezebel in the Old Testament was influenced by the spirit we call Jezebel today. She was practicing witchcraft—sorcery—against her enemies.

Jezebel's witchcraft can combat God's promise of divine health (see Isa. 53:4-5). Witchcraft can cause infirmity or masquerade as the spirit of infirmity to weaken your body so you can't walk in your highest calling. After all, when you feel sick or worn out it can be harder to do all you want to do for God because your flesh is severely weakened. Although His grace is sufficient, witchcraft is a powerful force that can take us off guard, and if we don't battle back we can find ourselves oppressed and ready to quit.

When witchcraft attacks me, my eyes burn. Sometimes my chest gets tight and I get dizzy. One of my intercessors gets terrible back pain when witchcraft manifests in her life. Another of my friends sees old stroke symptoms return. Sickness is not from God. We have authority over it, but many times we like to grumble and complain and confess how bad off we are, which only strengthens the enemy's grip on us.

Many times when I make an altar call for healing, the Holy Spirit shows me to break the powers of witchcraft off people's minds before praying over the infirmity that's attacking their bodies. The devil brings what Jonah 2:8 (KJV) calls "lying vanities" against you to make you think something is wrong so you'll confess it out of your mouth and open the door for the sickness to settle in. After this happened a few times, I decided to press in to discern the spiritual connection.

The Holy Spirit showed me that many times witchcraft against your mind can cause you to focus so much on the symptoms attacking your body that you can't extend your faith to receive God's healing power. In other words, if you aren't careful, when witchcraft attacks your mind you will wind up speaking and thinking about the infirmity rather than speaking and thinking about your healing, allowing the enemy to maintain the stronghold.

## HOW DOES THIS LITERALLY WORK?

Sometimes Jezebel accomplished her wicked agenda with unholy fasting. In Joel 1:14 (NIV), God told the prophet Joel, "Declare a holy fast." The enemy counterfeits everything God does. So if there is a holy fast, there is an unholy fast.

Part of the witchcraft that came against me was worked through an unholy fast. In looking back, this young prophet to whom we traced the curse that left me bedridden many days always said he was on a fast. It didn't realize it at the time, but the Holy Spirit gave me revelation afterward. He was on unholy fasts.

We see the concept of unholy fasts in the Bible. Remember when the Jews devised a plot to kill Paul the apostle? Acts 23:12-14 reads:

> *And when it was day, some of the Jews banded together and bound themselves under an oath, saying that they would neither eat nor drink till they had killed Paul. Now there were more than forty who had formed this conspiracy. They came to the chief priests and elders, and said, "We have bound ourselves under a great oath that we will eat nothing until we have killed Paul."*

This is pure witchcraft. But it's not the only time we see the concept in Scripture. Jezebel worked her witchcraft through an unholy fast. When Naboth refused to sell Ahab his field, the king became sullen and refused to eat. Jezebel found out about it and plotted against Naboth with an unholy fast. Observe this in 1 Kings 21:8-13:

> *And she wrote letters in Ahab's name, sealed them with his seal, and sent the letters to the elders and the nobles who were dwelling in the city with Naboth. She wrote in the letters, saying, "Proclaim a fast, and seat Naboth with high honor among the people; and seat two men, scoundrels, before him to bear witness against him, saying, 'You have blasphemed God and the king.' Then take him out, and stone him, that he may die."*
>
> *So the men of his city, the elders and nobles who were inhabitants of his city, did as Jezebel had sent to them, as it was written in the letters which she had sent to*

*them. They proclaimed a fast, and seated Naboth with high honor among the people. And two men, scoundrels, came in and sat before him; and the scoundrels witnessed against him, against Naboth, in the presence of the people, saying, "Naboth has blasphemed God and the king!" Then they took him outside the city and stoned him with stones, so that he died.*

The unholy fast against Paul did not prevail. The unholy fast against Naboth did. What was the difference? The unholy fast against Paul was exposed. Paul's nephew heard about it and told his uncle, who then sent him to the commander of the guards and told him what was going on. I'm sure Paul also prayed against it. The unholy fast orchestrated against me seemed to prosper for a time, but when it was exposed it was broken. An enemy exposed is an enemy defeated.

## JEZEBEL'S WITCHCRAFT WORD CURSES

Other times, Jezebel literally had her enemies murdered, like the true prophets of Jehovah who would not eat at her table. Still other times, she released word curses that sent people into fear and depression, as she did with Elijah after the showdown at Mount Carmel.

I believe people can release witchcraft word curses against you. I more than believe it, I know it because my inbox is full of them every week. People curse me, my family, my ministry, and more with the wicked words of their mouth—most of the time, these are Christians.

A witchcraft word curse from a Christian, I believe, is more powerful than any curse from a witch because a believer's words carry an anointing. We're supposed to break yokes with our words, but I believe we can release yokes of sickness with words like, "You're going to get sick if you don't slow down," or "Your mother has all of these autoimmune diseases and that's your future," or "God didn't really heal him from that disease. It was just in remission and now it's manifesting again."

Of course, these witchcraft curses don't have to come through Christians. The power of death and life are in every created human being's mouth. Well-meaning doctors can unknowingly release word curses over you while trying to offer a diagnosis. And, yes, witches can release negative thought forms and curses against you. I knew one brother who was cursed by a well-known prophet in Africa and turned up with rashes all over his body until the curses were finally broken.

Left unchecked, witchcraft infirmities can open the door to the spirit of death. Remember, the power of death is in the tongue. When Jezebel released a word curse over Elijah, he sat under a broom tree wishing he was dead. In agreement with the enemy's plans, the mighty miracle-working warrior actually prayed that he could die (see 1 Kings 19:4). That's intense!

Of course, Elijah did not die. God preserved him from the power of death that tried to take him out by the words of his very own mouth. But prophetic witchcraft is not always so easily broken. You can unknowingly welcome the power of death in your life by your thoughts and actions. The spirit of death is sneaky. You need to discern its operations before you can defeat it. Once you are sure you are battling this spirit, you can surely take authority over its operations.

## PROPHETIC-PSYCHIC ATTACKS

When I was writing *The Spiritual Warrior's Guide to Defeating Water Spirits*, I was also heavily attacked by prophetic witchcraft through a python spirit. If you've never heard of a python spirit, let me show it to you in the Bible.

You'll find it in Acts 16:16 when Paul encounters a girl possessed with a spirit of divination. The word for *divination* in this verse comes from the Greek word *puthon*, which translates in English as *python*. *Vine's Dictionary* explains how Greek mythology believed the Pythian serpent guarded the oracle of Delphi until Apollo slew it (and then took on the name Pythian). The word was later applied to diviners or soothsayers inspired by Apollo.

When writing the water spirits book, a psychic or psychological attack, came with the physical attack I offered this account in the book:

> While writing the first two chapters of this book, I took one of the hardest spiritual warfare hits of my life—and I'm no battlefield novice. It seemed to come out of absolutely nowhere, but it was a high-level tactical plan against my destiny.
>
> I woke up on Sunday morning feeling stiff in my body, with a whopping migraine headache. My state of mind could best be described as a scrambled egg. I could not string together two thoughts because the vain imaginations were hitting my mind in rapid-fire succession. Before I could cast one down, another

took its place. It's as if the demon powers were competing with one another as to who could deliver the knockout punch.

The overarching emotion that worked to overwhelm my soul was defeat, then disgust, the desperation for breakthrough. My chest grew tight. I had a difficult time breathing. My heart started pounding. I stood. I paced. I sat. I warred. I praised. I called for intercessory prayer backup. I did everything I'd been taught to do, but dizziness gripped my head and I felt like no oxygen was getting to my brain.

Somehow, in my determination I made it to church but I had no idea how I was going to preach the Word. In the back office, I started chocking. I was not overcome, but I was daze and confused. I was never once afraid, but I was angry. At one point, I felt powerless to break through the attack. Thank God, I had an intercessor standing with me that went in deep.

I had never experienced anything like it before and hope never to again—it was just that intense. As my intercessor prayed, she began shaking with righteous indignation. I literally felt the enemy loose my body and my mind.

When I say literally, I mean literally. One moment I was in physical and mind distress. The next minute I was free and clear and felt completely normal. Yes, just like that. I am still learning from the experience, though I am certain several water spirits formed a confederate to attack me—backlash from exposing this wicked demonic underbelly.[1]

## HOW PSYCHIC-PROPHETIC ATTACKS WORK

If you are suffering from depression, anxiety, bipolar disorder, schizophrenia, or uncontrollable emotions, you could be battling advanced demonic oppression. It could be witchcraft. You may experience a wide spectrum of emotions such as deep discouragement, the need to control everything, self-pity, fear, and extreme loneliness. You may have trouble sleeping. These are not normal behaviors or emotions for blood-bought, born-again Christians.

Some years ago, as I was praying to break word curses, the Holy Spirit reminded me of the reality of thought curses. One of my prophetic mentors instructed me about fifteen years ago that someone was releasing thought curses against me and it was causing me emotional distress. I forgot all about that until the Holy Spirit brought it back up again—and then I found theology to back up the theory.

The preacher said, "Even in your mind do not curse the king; and in your bedchamber do not curse the rich; for a bird in the sky may carry your voice, and a winged creature may declare the matter" (Eccl. 10:20 MEV).

The word *curse* in that Scripture means, "to make despicable, to curse, to make light, to treat with contempt, bring contempt, or dishonor," according to *The KJV Old Testament Hebrew Lexicon*. The Bible says even in your mind—another translation says in your thoughts—not to curse people. Even in your mind! A word curse gives voice to an evil thought, but how can a thought take voice in the spirit realm?

Have you ever walked into a room and the atmosphere was tense or gloomy? And then when you speak to the person in the room, you discover they are tense or gloomy. Could it be possible that their thoughts have impacted the atmosphere in the room? I believe so. I believe if thoughts are powerful to change our own mind, they must be powerful enough to change the atmosphere around us and may be powerful enough to release witchcraft at people.

What I do know is this: witches believe in negative thought forms. Negative thought forms are described as "structured inter-dimensional energy" that witches work up against victims for a specific purpose. These are intentional psychic attacks that come through negative thinking, jealousy, anger, fear, revenge, and other negative thoughts. If there is power in positive thinking, there must be power in negative thinking.

## TAKING AUTHORITY OVER WITCHCRAFT MENTAL AND EMOTIONAL INFIRMITIES

What's a believer to do? When it comes to witchcraft, we have to withstand it. The Amplified Bible, Classic Edition says to "be firm in faith [against his onset—rooted, established, strong, immovable, and determined]" (1 Pet. 5:9). It's easy enough to give in to witchcraft, especially if you don't know what is attacking you.

Remember, although people may be releasing prophetic witchcraft over you, our fight is not with flesh and blood. The people who are targeting you are themselves wrapped up in witchcraft and deceived. They are merely Jezebel's puppets.

So if you feel like giving up, when you feel tired for no reason, when you have strong confusion, when you are fighting an intense battle in your mind, and when infirmities are manifesting, it could be witchcraft—and it could lead you to the doorstep of infirmity. Resist it at its onset. Cast it off. Submit yourself to God. "Resist the devil [stand firm against him], and he will flee from you" (James 4:7 AMPC).

Put on the whole armor and engage in the battle. Passivity isn't going to deliver you from Jezebel's witchcraft. Remember 2 Corinthians 10:3-6 (MEV):

> *For though we walk in the flesh, we do not war according to the flesh. For the weapons of our warfare are not carnal, but mighty through God to the pulling down of strongholds, casting down imaginations and every high thing that exalts itself against the knowledge of God, bringing every thought into captivity to the obedience of Christ, and being ready to punish all disobedience when your obedience is complete.*

Take authority over the witchcraft in the name above all names. But before you do, make sure you don't have any common ground with the enemy. Repent for any rebellion in your heart, and surrender your will anew to God. Thank Jesus for His blood and plead it over yourself. Rejoice in the Lord. Praise and worship carry breakthrough. That's often all it takes to change the spiritual climate in your home. And worship is where we should start because He is worthy of our adoration. Check out my book *Cleansing Your Home from Evil* to root out hidden demonic influences.

If worship doesn't break the witchcraft, keep binding it. Witchcraft has to bow at the name of Jesus. Remember, we are more than conquerors in Christ and no weapon formed against us can prosper—not even witchcraft. Our job is to be spiritually discerning enough to catch the devil at his onset, resist him, rebuke him, and praise God for the victory.

Don't underestimate the power of praying in tongues to find deliverance from prophetic witchcraft. The power of the Holy Spirit delivers you. Romans 8:26 (KJV) tells us, "Likewise the Spirit also helpeth our infirmities: for we know not what we should pray for as we ought: but the Spirit itself maketh intercession for us with groanings which cannot be uttered." Yield your tongue to the Spirit of Life. Cry out in tongues for deliverance from prophetic witchcraft's ailments.

As Christians, we need to obey Scripture. Second Corinthians 10:5-6 (MEV) talks about casting down imaginations, but we often forget the part that says to bring "every thought into captivity to the obedience of Christ, and being ready to punish all disobedience when your obedience is complete."

Combating thought curses starts with our own thoughts. If we're cursing ourselves in our thoughts, we need to intentionally think the opposite of what the enemy is telling us, what people say about us, or what we think about our own shortcomings. We need to declare the truth out of our mouths. By the same token, we need to guard our thoughts about others. We don't want to be used of the enemy against anyone and violate the law of love.

Remember, we are more than conquerors in Christ, and no weapon formed against us can prosper—not even witchcraft. Our job is to be spiritually discerning enough to catch the devil at his onset, resist him, rebuke him, and praise God for the victory. Sometimes the battle is fiercer and longer than we would like to endure, but we will win if we don't quit.

CHAPTER 9

# DELIVERANCE FROM FALSE PROPHETIC ALIGNMENTS, CHURCHES, AND

# NETWORKS

**M**y coach called it emotional terrorism and psychological warfare. I had never heard such terms, but when these methods were explained to me, I had an "aha" moment.

Let me back up a moment. I had just signed up for a coaching program so I could see what I couldn't see in the realm of business growth and personal leadership development. When I enrolled in the program, I had absolutely no idea that I would soon be breaking false prophetic alignments and leaving a church and network steeped in prophetic witchcraft.

But, again, let me back up a moment. I was in a prophetic church for eight years that went wonky somewhere around the fifth year. I was a single mother operating my freelance writing practice out of my home, but also served on the church's leadership staff and handled the media efforts as a volunteer. I basically worked forty hours a week for myself and forty hours a week at the church. The more I gave, the more was expected until it became too much.

The "too much" started with a demand for quarterly lunch meetings to discuss media. These meetings were hard for me to make, since I was always on news deadlines and the lunches were literally three hours long. I sucked it up and went. But then it turned into weekly staff meetings on Monday mornings. It was nearly impossible for me to make this work. I went a couple of times and just could not continuing compromising my livelihood. One Monday, I woke up with a stye in my eye and a headache on top of my impending deadlines, so I informed the administrator I would not make the meeting.

I'll always remember getting a phone call from the apostle indicating that if I didn't drive up to the church immediately, I would be "fired" from my volunteer position. He also had a few other choice words for me, including several curses. The intimidating prophetic witchcraft literally made me sick to my stomach. I never went to another Monday meeting again, nor did he kick me off the staff. I was too valuable, given the many hours of free labor. It was an empty threat. Prophetic witchcraft often is.

Fast-forward another year and the church held a concert for a member putting out an album. I was on a Friday nights sabbatical to spend that time with my then-teenaged daughter. The apostle wanted me to attend the event and handle the media. I told them—and they already knew long before this—that I had set this season of Friday nights aside for my daughter but would make sure my team handled it. And so I did. My team performed with excellence. The following Sunday morning, the apostle gave me the cold shoulder. He avoided me until the leadership meeting after church and then he let me have it.

## TORN UP AND TORN DOWN

In front of about fifty people, he tore me up, made false accusations, and spewed anger my way. His false accusations claimed I was AWOL and was in dereliction of duty. He knew that was not true but for fifteen minutes raved, raged and cursed me prolifically in front of the rest of the staff. I was told I had no anointing and that any success I enjoyed was purely due to his anointing. I was told that if I left the church I would wander in the wilderness the rest of my life. I was told all that and more.

Sadly, my first instinct was to try harder. I didn't see the level of deception I was in. So I did try harder. But it was never enough. Nothing I did after that was ever good enough. They told me I had a Jezebel spirit and was deceived. At that point, I knew I was deceived but I didn't know if they were deceiving me or if I was deceiving myself. That's when I got outside counsel from some pastors who told me it was prophetic abuse in its most classic form and that I should leave the church immediately.

One night, I was praying through this advice and the Holy Spirit instructed me to forgive everyone in the church for everything they had ever done to me. He took me down a list of offenses, some of which I didn't even recognize as offenses at the time. I was so young in the Lord when I got to that church, I didn't know what church was supposed to be like. I didn't know how wrong their behavior really was. After about an hour of forgiving, forgiving, and forgiving some more, the Holy Spirit told me, "Go in peace."

Of course, I tried to go in peace but they wouldn't let me. They made videos about me, calling me a false prophet. They told the church I had Jezebel, python, and Leviathan spirits. They said that I had turned my back on Christ and was going to hell. Everyone in the church was warned never to speak to me again, lest I lead them into a pit of deception. I lost every friend I had. Over ten years later, people still come to my church, Awakening House of Prayer in Fort Lauderdale, who were also hurt in that abusive environment. They tell me they found me because this apostle still trashes my name. They figure I survived the prophetic witchcraft and maybe I can help them too.

## WHY WE PUT UP WITH PROPHETIC TERRORISM

Have you ever wondered why people put up with prophetic terrorism, psychological warfare, and other forms of spiritual abuse? There are many reasons. I am thoroughly convinced I was supposed to leave the church that was slowly stripping me of my identity two years before I finally woke up.

At first, I didn't know it was abuse. As I said, I was such a new believer that I didn't know what church was supposed to look like. I only knew what I was taught. But as I grew in my knowledge of the Word of God, something about the church didn't seem right. The church never preached on love or the fruit of the Spirit and both were sorely lacking. The leaders labeled people and shunned many who threatened them before they even got all the way through the front door. Sometimes, we are ignorant of what abuse in a religious context looks like.

Later, I was told I was misreading the situation. I was told I was misinterpreting events. This is a gaslighting technique. Gaslighting is psychological manipulation of a person usually over an extended time period that causes the victim to question the validity of their own thoughts, perception of reality, or memories. Gaslighting typically leads to confusion, loss of confidence and self-esteem, uncertainty of one's emotional or mental stability, and a dependency on the perpetrator, according to *Merriam-Webster*'s dictionary.

That's a mouthful right there. Learn the catchphrases of gaslighters and even if you lack discernment you'll see through it. Gaslighting catchphrases may sound like this: Stop being so sensitive. That never happened. Why can't you take a joke? Stop exaggerating. It wasn't that bad. Why can't you let go of the past? You're acting crazy. You need help. That's not what I meant. You don't need to get so upset about this. And so on. Get the picture?

In my case, all my friends and ministry opportunities were in the church. We have to be careful that our desire for friends and community doesn't take a higher position in our lives than the voice of the friend who sticks closer than a brother—Jesus. We can't value the comfort of people more than we value the comfort of the Comforter—the Holy Spirit. Leaving a church or network doesn't mean you are leaving God.

I stayed at that abusive church longer than I should have because leaving meant I was losing my friends, front row seat, teaching platform, and more. For others, it's the reality that their whole family goes to the abusive church and are all under the haze of deception. The family can't see it so you feel stuck. You don't want to deal with the family drama. Sometimes we stay because we don't know where else we would go if we left, or because we're afraid of what would happen to us. At the church I left, I watched them crucify everyone with any visibility who left. For a long time, that was an incentive not to leave.

Some people stay in abusive churches because society drives the ride-or-die concept into our minds. Church drills the words *covenant* and *loyalty* into your mind. Your values can keep you in a dangerous place. You can have angst over feeling like you are violating your values or vows. Let me set you free: you don't need to maintain loyalty to someone who is working for the enemy. Your first pledge of allegiance needs to go to Jesus. He will tell you who to run with and who to escape from.

One of the most common reasons people stay aligned to ministries operating in prophetic witchcraft is because they think things will change if they stay and pay. One minister in the same church I left saw all the signs and was grieved. She went into the pastor's office and told him she saw "Ichabod" written in the spirit over the church. She warned if the leadership didn't change its ways God's glory would leave. She was rebuked, stripped of all her responsibilities in the church, and still felt obligated to stay there and pray away the deception. I have never seen that work. Know this: you can pray from the outside for those on the inside.

## EXITING PROPHETIC WITCHCRAFT'S STRONG GRIP

So how do you get out, then? Find someone on the outside whom you can trust. Talk to them about your experience without operating in bitter dishonor. I had a pastor friend who was retired. His name was Pastor Mike. Pastor Mike ministered to me for months and connected me to another pastor in Cincinnati who really helped me see the dynamics of the prophetic witchcraft.

The Cincinnati pastor pointed me to 1 Thessalonians. Inspired by the Holy Spirit, Paul the apostle wrote:

> *But we behaved gently when we were among you, like a devoted mother nursing and cherishing her own children. So, being thus tenderly and affectionately desirous of you, we continued to share with you not only God's good news (the Gospel) but also our own lives as well, for you had become so very dear to us* (1 Thessalonians 2:7-8 AMPC).

These verses made the abuse painfully obvious. I had to accept the truth about what was happening. I could no longer deny it. I had a clear choice: I could stay under this spell until I was so deceived I started deceiving others, or I could walk away and walk in the truth that set me free. I decided to walk out with truth on my side.

I left in peace—quietly—like the Holy Spirit told me to do. Within weeks, others started leaving. Within a year, other leaders started leaving. Sometimes, you are the catalyst for others' freedom. Some of the people who shunned me and cursed me on the way out the door came to me for help. This was part of the Lord's vindication. Keep in mind, I didn't try to rescue the people who were left behind. That was not my job. I obeyed the Holy Spirit's instruction to go in peace.

## GET READY FOR WITCHCRAFT'S RETALIATION

Expect retaliation when you leave. Prophetic terrorists are big into public humiliation, which is what I and many other people experienced at the toxic church we left. Public humiliation is a form of punishment through shaming, dishonoring, and disgracing words. This was a common practice at the church I escaped.

Then there's the cold shoulder or the silent treatment. When we try to punish others with the silent treatment; when we work to manipulate people with tears and pouting so they will feel guilty; when we intimidate people we are essentially practicing a form of witchcraft and idolatry. Prophetic terrorists also make threats and engage in mental abuse.

Some of the women at the church even tried to turn my teenaged daughter against me, coming to my house when they knew I wasn't home. They knocked on the door and tried to get her to come out and talk to them. When that didn't work, they continued to call my daughter and tell her lies about me. One of the ladies in the church said I was an unfit mother for removing my daughter from the youth group and insinuated social services needed to get involved.

At first, all this seemed to be working. My daughter's friends were in the church and she did not want to leave. At one point, she told me she would walk the three miles to church if she had to. But the enemy always overplays his hand. Eventually these meddling church members crossed the line and my daughter discerned the motives. The enemy's plan backfired. Now, she refers to the church as a cult.

Emotional terrorism goes hand in hand with psychological warfare. The *Merriam-Webster* definition is "things that are done to make someone (such as an enemy or opponent) become less confident or feel hopeless, afraid, etc." The text messages telling me I had demons were nonstop. My mentor at the church told me I was merciless and unforgiving. The Facebook posts with subtle messages were hurtful. At one point, I started second guessing my decision to leave. My coach, who got more than he bargained for, told me to cut off all communication in every mode. I did. And that's when I began to find true deliverance from prophetic witchcraft.

## OVERCOMING WITCHCRAFT'S HURT

Physically removing yourself from a church, alignment, or network steeped with prophetic witchcraft is an important step in deliverance. But it's only the first step. Deliverance from prophetic witchcraft also means healing the wounds prophetic witchcraft inflicted on your soul through emotional terrorism and psychological warfare.

Prophetic witchcraft wounds us when the love people have for us is conditional upon some type of performance or behavior—whether that's attendance, giving, or serving. When you stop performing, you start meeting with punishment. Prophetic witchcraft wounds happen through rejection, ostracization, neglect, public humiliation, and false accusations.

I recall the church I was at working me to death. I was picking up the graphic designer's slack on a project time and time again. That meant early mornings and late nights while he slept. I was so exhausted and fed up at one point that I resigned. The leaders swarmed on me, hoping to get me back under their thumb. They talked me into coming back, but little did I know they would put me on probation as if I was the problem. The apostle called me unstable and said I would never succeed in life with this attitude. He said he would be watching me. After about six months, he said, "You made it. I didn't think you would make it."

So how do you overcome the pain prophetic witchcraft inflicted? First, acknowledge the hurt. Don't pretend you are okay because you are not okay. Don't bury the pain. Pain buried alive never dies. Take it to God in prayer. When prophetic witchcraft wounds you, run to your prayer closet. Ask God to heal you. Psalm 34:18 (NIV) promises, "The Lord is close to the brokenhearted and saves those who are crushed in spirit." And Psalm 147:3 encourages, "He heals the brokenhearted and binds up their wounds."

## TAKE THE PAIN TO GOD

When prophetic witchcraft wounds you, the very first action to take is prayer. The hurt you feel is real and pretending like you aren't hurt isn't going to bring healing. Sometimes when we get hurt in church, folks like to tell us that we have no reason to feel bad and we just need to get over it. Half of that statement is true. We do need to get over it, but it's not always true that we have no reason to feel bad. If someone is spewing malicious gossip behind your back and you find out about it, it stings.

Whatever you do, don't rush into a confrontation with the offender. Take it to God in prayer. Psalm 50:15 says, "Call upon me in the day of trouble." That works for a troubled soul just as well as it does any other trouble. Tell Him how you feel and ask Him to heal your wounds. It may be that the Lord is going to deal with the offender directly and anything you say would just make matters worse. Or, it could be that the Lord will give you a graceful way to explain why you feel hurt. If you take it to God, He can give you the very words to say to your offender (see Luke 12:12). And He can bring conviction to that person's heart when you approach them with a spirit of humility (see John 16:8).

But know this—the healing can't begin until you forgive. That's why the Holy Spirit had me spend an hour forgiving all those who hurt me before He gave me the green light to leave the church. The Lord commands us to forgive. Paul wrote in Colossians 3:13 (ESV), "Bearing with one another and, if one has a complaint against another, forgiving each other; as the Lord has forgiven you, so you also must forgive."

The bottom line is this: it doesn't matter how wrong your offender is, you have to forgive. Forgiveness is not for the other person—it's for you. Forgiveness doesn't justify what someone did that was wrong, nor does it necessarily mean that the relationship goes right back to where it was.

If you don't forgive, you end up bitter and resentful and before too long you'll end up hurting other people. The healing process can't really begin until you spit out the bait of offense. I'll leave you with this prophetic insight the Holy Spirit gave me once when I was extremely hurt in church:

> *"When the feeling of hurt arises, the spirit of offense comes on the scene to fortify the pain, tempting you to hold on to the grudge in your heart. Therefore, the proper response to emotional pain of the soul is always*

*an immediate confession of forgiveness from the heart. The alternative to forgiveness from the heart is the ongoing torment of the soul. So if you want to be free from your hurts and wounds, take thoughts of forgiveness, meditate on them, and confess them rather than taking thoughts of the hurt, meditating on them, and confessing them. This is God's way—and it's the only way that brings true healing. And, while you are at it, pray for those who have hurt you. This process will cleanse your heart and renew your mind. And you will walk free from the pain of your past."*

Amen.

## DON'T LOOK BACK

When we realize prophetic witchcraft has victimized us, we often replay the incident in our head over and over and over. We waver between whether we were just imagining these offenses or if they actually happened. Then we get angry because we know it was real.

Let me give you some practical advice: stop rehashing the incident. Cast down the thoughts of the past rather than dwelling on them. Some reflection is helpful in processing to learn valuable lessons but too much can create a tipping point in your soul where you feel stuck. There's a fine line. Don't cross it. Determine get over it and you will. Then you can be an agent of deliverance in someone else's life.

## DON'T RETALIATE

Whatever you do, don't retaliate. In His Sermon on the Mount, Jesus teaches us to turn the other cheek (see Matt. 5:39) and to love our enemies, bless those who curse us, do good to those who hate us, and pray for those who spitefully use us and persecute us (see Matt. 5:44).

With that in mind, don't go around telling everybody what someone did to hurt your feelings. And don't make accusations against those who hurt you if you decide to confront the matter. Instead of saying, "You hurt my feelings!" say, "When you did that I felt hurt" or "When you talk to me like that I feel upset." Own your feelings because they are your feelings. It's very possible that your offender has no idea that what they said or did hurt you—and never meant to hurt you. If you approach them in humility seeking reconciliation, your offender may be quick to apologize.

God wants to vindicate your pain, so don't retaliate. Return good for evil. When you get delivered from the church, alignment, or network that held you back and held you down, don't go back and tell the whole group they are deceived. You are not Holy Ghost, Junior. Just pray for the ones who hurt you—and pray for the ones you left behind. I did this for years and saw many people come out of the toxic cultish church I was part of. Jesus said in Luke 6:28 (NIV), "Bless those who curse you, pray for those who mistreat you."

## YOU MAY NEED COUNSELING

You may need Christian counseling to rid yourself of the toxins prophetic witchcraft left behind. If you have issues with authority, you need help. I couldn't trust leaders for a long time after my experience. I was always scared to death or thought I was in trouble if a leader called me wanting to talk. I also had trust issues with the church at large. I tried to find a place to fit in, but my discernment was sometimes clouded by paranoia and anytime I saw anything that smelled like control I fled.

I struggled with guilt, shame, and condemnation for a season. I was unable to receive the grace or love of God because this was not taught or modeled to me. I had to unlearn wrong things I was taught. The good news is, Jesus is a Wonderful Counselor (see Isa. 9:6). If you don't have anyone to turn to as you exit prophetic witchcraft, know that Jesus will hide you under the shadow of His wings—and there is healing in His wings.

# NOTE

1.   Jennifer LeClaire, *The Spiritual Warrior's Guide to Defeating Water Spirits* (Shippensburg, PA: Destiny Image Publishers, 2018), 37-38.

# CHAPTER 10

# DETOXING
# YOUR SOUL

**W**e always covered the apostle in prayer when he traveled. We covered his home, his family, his finances—he had 360-degree prayer. We were determined to stand in the gap for him and were faithful to pray without ceasing. Still, despite all the prayer, his house was flooded during a massive rainstorm. The enemy came in like a flood, literally.

Of course, his house was not the only one on the block to suffer damages. It was a major storm, and because he was in a low-lying area, all the homes were flooded. Somehow, though, we took the blame. He was fighting mad when he got home and decided it was our fault. It defied reasoning, seeing as we were praying and the flooding was not unprecedented. It happens.

As a result, the apostle called us all to repentance. I was fairly young in the Lord and I just couldn't wrap my mind around how this was our fault. Before I could even process it, the elder prophet in the church called us all into the back room and led us into repentance for allowing such a terrible thing to happen to the man of God.

Then, suddenly, she pronounced shame on us. She said, "Lord, send your shame on us to bear for seven days!" I suppose she was working from Numbers 12:14 where the Lord suggested that Miriam should be shamed seven days after she and Aaron spoke against Moses. Perhaps this prophet forgot that Jesus bore our shame.

Well, the devil took advantage of that prophet's words. I could literally see the countenance on the faces of the other intercessors as shame descended on the group. She invited the enemy upon us, and we received it. I immediately felt oppressed, embarrassed, like I didn't even have a right to join the leadership meeting that followed the prayer meeting. I went home feeling ashamed.

Shame is a real emotion that we may feel when we do something wrong. But it's not God's will for us to walk in shame. If we feel ashamed, we can repent, ask for forgiveness, and move on in the grace of God. If we do something shameful, we turn away from it. We can renounce the hidden things of shame (see 2 Cor. 4:2). When I got home, the Lord put a spotlight on a book that was in my library—one I had never read. There was a chapter called "Betrayal and Shame." I started reading at about 7 p.m. I read and prayed until about 2 a.m., and the Lord opened my eyes and delivered me from that shame the prophet pronounced.

## DEALING WITH TOXIC EMOTIONS

When I escaped prophetic witchcraft—even after I broke soul ties—I still had to deal with toxic emotions. As I've shared with you, I was taught wrong about some things. I was word-cursed. I was called names. Even after I left, I was persecuted, lied about, and more. I was in a whirlwind of emotions—and many of them were toxic. I was angry. I was hurt. I was wounded. I was traumatized. Deliverance from these toxic emotions meant a soul detox.

A soul detox is ridding your mind, will, emotions, imagination, reasonings, and intellect from toxins and impurities. Just like a liver or colon detox removes foreign substances that keep your organs from functioning at optimal levels, a soul detox delivers you from wrong thoughts, beliefs, and teachings that keep you oppressed. Essentially, its being "renewed in the spirit of your mind" (Eph. 4:23).

If every believer needs mind renewal—and we do—then how much more does the victim of prophetic witchcraft need a soul detox? With the lies and deception, with the rejection and shame, with the intimidation and flattery, prophetic witchcraft can warp the soul. Thanks be to God, He makes the crooked places straight even in our mind. Paul instructed:

> *I beseech you therefore, brethren, by the mercies of God, that you present your bodies a living sacrifice, holy, acceptable to God, which is your reasonable service. And do not be conformed to this world, but be transformed by the renewing of your mind, that you may prove what is that good and acceptable and perfect will of God* (Romans 12:1-2).

You could put it this way: don't let prophetic witchcraft continue to shape your thinking. Let God transform your mind, will, imaginations, reasonings, and intellect to His way of thinking. Choose to focus on godly values and ethical attitudes. Let words of life heal your soul, reset your thinking and you will experience a metamorphosis. You will be stronger and wiser than before because what the enemy meant for harm God is going to work out for your good (see Gen. 50:20).

## CASTING DOWN CARNAL THINKING

Detoxing your soul from prophetic witchcraft starts with casting down carnal thinking. Carnal thinking is self-centered. Carnal thinking wants more, more, and more. Carnal thinking rejects any notion of forgiveness. Carnal thinking makes people into idols. Carnal thinking creates an internal war. Carnal thinking operates by sight and not faith. Paul offered a clear warning in Romans 8:5-7:

> *For those who live according to the flesh set their minds on the things of the flesh, but those who live according to the Spirit, the things of the Spirit. For to be carnally minded is death, but to be spiritually minded is life and peace. Because the carnal mind is enmity against God; for it is not subject to the law of God, nor indeed can be.*

Since carnal thinking was the open door that allowed prophetic witchcraft to deceive you, a soul detox starts with trading carnal thinking for the mind of Christ. Paul said, "Let this mind be in you which was also in Christ Jesus" (Phil. 2:5). The sooner we realize there is nothing to be gained in God's Kingdom through fleshly thoughts, feelings, and actions, the sooner we can rid our souls of the impact of prophetic witchcraft, which is both carnal and demonic.

There is no good thing in our flesh. In fact, Paul made this very clear in Galatians 5:17 (NLT):

> *The sinful nature wants to do evil, which is just the opposite of what the Spirit wants. And the Spirit gives us desires that are the opposite of what the sinful nature desires. These two forces are constantly fighting each other, so you are not free to carry out your good intentions."*

## CASTING DOWN IMAGINATIONS

While you are working out your soul detox, the enemy is sure to come at you with imaginations. The apostle Paul gives this instruction to the church at Corinth, which was in many ways carnally minded:

> *Casting down arguments and every high thing that exalts itself against the knowledge of God, bringing every thought into captivity to the obedience of Christ, and being ready to punish all disobedience when your obedience is fulfilled* (2 Corinthians 10:5-6).

The Amplified Bible, Classic Edition breaks it down in finer detail:

> *[Inasmuch as we] refute arguments and theories and reasonings and every proud and lofty thing that sets itself up against the [true] knowledge of God; and we lead every thought and purpose away captive into the obedience of Christ (the Messiah, the Anointed One), being in readiness to punish every [insubordinate for his] disobedience, when your own submission and obedience [as a church] are fully secured and complete.*

Prophetic witchcraft exalted itself against the knowledge of God in your soul—and you want to punish those demons that left you in bondage. Keep in mind, casting down imaginations is a violent spiritual exercise that must be verbalized. The phrase "casting down" in 2 Corinthians 10:5 comes from the Greek word *kathaireó*, which has a violent connotation. According to *The KJV New Testament Greek Lexicon*, *kathaireó* means to "forcibly yank down; destroy, leaving nothing 'standing' or even in good working order; cast down." It also means to cast down with the use of force.

When the enemy comes to sow wrong thoughts into your soul, run to the battle line in your mind and cast them down. Remember, the battle is in the mind, but the war is for your heart. Here's a practical example. When you hear thoughts like, "I shouldn't have broken covenant with the prophet," you know that's prophetic witchcraft trying to get you to return to bondage like the Israelites wanted to return to Egypt. Recognize it as a vain imagination that is working to exalt itself above God's will in your life and speak to it out loud. Say, "I reject the lie that I should return to the prophet (or whatever person or ministry is involved). I bind this imagination and cast it down, in Jesus' name. I am free to follow Christ the prophet." As I wrote in my book, *101 Tactics for Spiritual Warfare*:

> The idea is you never cast down without lifting up the Word of God. You don't bind without loosing. You don't just eradicate a wrong thought; you replace it with the right thought. You may have to do this over and over again with fearful thoughts because we never defeat fear once and for all. Fear is always roaming about like a roaring lion looking to devour your wild dreams. But you can submit yourself to God, resist fear, and force it to flee (see James 4:7).[1]

## CULTIVATING SPIRITUAL-MINDEDNESS

Of course, it's not enough to strip yourself of carnal-mindedness. The idea is to be spiritually minded. Again, Paul writes, "Now the mind of the flesh [which is sense and reason without the Holy Spirit] is death [death that comprises all the miseries arising from sin, both here and hereafter]. But the mind of the [Holy] Spirit is life and [soul] peace [both now and forever]" (Rom. 8:6 AMPC).

So how do you develop spiritual-mindedness? Paul offers nine keys in Philippians 4:8:

*Finally, brethren, whatever things are true, whatever things are noble, whatever things are just, whatever things are pure, whatever things are lovely, whatever things are of good report, if there is any virtue and if there is anything praiseworthy—meditate on these things.*

That means if it's not true, noble, just, pure, lovely, of a good report, virtuous, or praiseworthy, you shouldn't be thinking it. But if it is true, noble, just, pure, lovely, of a good report, virtuous, or praiseworthy, you should meditate on it. Meditating on the Word—not just reading it but really thinking through it, praying through it, confessing it, and even imagining it—renews the mind. God's ways are higher than our ways and His thoughts are higher than our thoughts (see Isa. 55:8-9), but when we think according to Paul's guidelines we are thinking like the Spirit of God and, therefore, becoming more spiritually minded.

God spoke these pivotal words to Joshua:

*This Book of the Law shall not depart from your mouth, but you shall meditate in it day and night, that you may observe to do according to all that is written in it. For then you will make your way prosperous, and then you will have good success. Have I not commanded you? Be strong and of good courage; do not be afraid, nor be dismayed, for the Lord your God is with you wherever you go* (Joshua 1:8-9).

I like to look at various translations of Philippians 4:8 to drive home the point. *The Voice* puts it this way: "fill your minds with beauty and truth." Our God is beautiful and so is His truth. The Amplified Bible says this:

> *whatever is honorable and worthy of respect, whatever is right and confirmed by God's word, whatever is pure and wholesome, whatever is lovely and brings peace, whatever is admirable and of good repute; if there is any excellence, if there is anything worthy of praise, think continually on these things [center your mind on them, and implant them in your heart].*

I love that. Center your mind on them and implant them in your heart.

## SET YOUR MIND ON THINGS ABOVE

Another aspect of being spiritually minded is to set your mind on things above. Paul offers this Spirit-inspired wisdom in Colossians 3:1-2: "If then you were raised with Christ, seek those things which are above, where Christ is, sitting at the right hand of God. Set your mind on things above, not on things on the earth." The New Living Translation offers: "Think about the things of heaven, not the things of earth." And the Amplified Bible puts it this way: "Set your mind and keep focused habitually on the things above [the heavenly things], not on things that are on the earth [which have only temporal value]."

Remember when Peter rebuked Jesus for saying He would die on a cross? Jesus returned the rebuke with these words: "Get behind

Me, Satan! You are an offense to Me, for you are not mindful of the things of God, but the things of men" (Matt. 16:23). Just a few moments earlier, when Peter was spiritually minded, he received a revelation that Jesus was the Christ. As soon as he took his mind off the things above, he slipped into carnal thinking. This demonstrates the discipline it takes to keep your mind set on things above. It takes work, especially at first.

What does it mean to keep your mind set on things above? For starters, remember that your citizenship is in heaven (see Phil. 3:20). The writer of Hebrews expounded on this:

> So let us go out to him beyond the city walls (that is, outside the interests of this world, being willing to be despised) to suffer with him there, bearing his shame. For this world is not our home; we are looking forward to our everlasting home in heaven (Hebrews 13:13-14 TLB).

We are in the world but not of the world and greater is He who is in us than he (the devil) that is in the world (see 1 John 4:4). John also wrote, "We know that we are of God, and the whole world lies under the sway of the wicked one" (1 John 5:19). We are not under the enemy's power legally, but when we set our minds on the things of the earth and the ways of the world, we give him an open door to our minds. We must be careful to guard our hearts with all diligence.

# GUARD YOUR HEART DILIGENTLY

We would do well to remember the wise words of Solomon in Proverbs 23:7, "For as he thinks in his heart, so is he." The idea is that our thoughts transform us, so we need to be careful what we think. Along those same lines, Solomon also wrote, "Guard your heart above all else, for it determines the course of your life" (Prov. 4:23 NLT).

Peter warns us to, "Gird up the loins of your mind, be sober, and rest your hope fully upon the grace that is to be brought to you at the revelation of Jesus Christ" (1 Pet. 1:13). Another way to say that is, "minds that are alert and fully sober" (NIV) or "prepare your minds for action and exercise self-control" (NLT) or "prepare your minds for action, be completely sober [in spirit—steadfast, self-disciplined, spiritually and morally alert]" (AMP).

So how do we guard our thoughts diligently? Well, there are some practical measures. And as you can see, it takes intention on your part. The word *diligence* demands work. *Diligence* means "steady, earnest, and energetic effort: devoted and painstaking work and application to accomplish and undertaking." It will require effort on your part to guard your mind, but it gets easier over time. Here are some practical tips.

Be careful what preachers you listen to. Their teachings are penetrating your ear gates and impacting your soul. That may be how you got into the prophetic witchcraft mess to begin with. Not everyone with a megachurch or large social media platform or measure of charisma is authentic. The number of followers doesn't validate truth. And as we go deeper into the end times, it's just going to get worse. (Check out my course, "Escaping the Great

End Times Deception" at www.schoolofthespirit.tv/deception.) By the same token, be careful of the entertainment you consume. Limit your exposure to negative people. Memorize Scripture. Put on your helmet of salvation, which guards your heart and mind in Christ Jesus (see Eph. 6:17).

## TOTAL MIND FREEDOM IS AVAILABLE

You can detox your soul from prophetic witchcraft. It will take consistent effort on your end, but all things are possible to the one who believes (see Mark 9:23). As you read the Word, ask the Holy Spirit to reveal to you any lie you are believing. Trust in Psalm 119:105, "Your word is a lamp to my feet and a light to my path." The Holy Spirit will show you where you went wrong in your thinking.

Don't let the notion of being deceived offend you. The nature of deception is that you don't know you are deceived. Even though at this point you know there's deception plaguing your soul, you may not know the specific lie holding you in bondage. Or you may know exactly where your soul is stuck.

Light always overcomes darkness. Jesus said, "The light shines in the darkness, and the darkness can never extinguish it" (John 1:5 NLT). Ask the Holy Spirit to break in with light so you can turn from darkness back to light and from the power of Satan to God. Ask Him to shine a light on any deception, error, heresy, or delusion in your soul and to root it out. Paul assures us, "Now the Lord is the Spirit; and where the Spirit of the Lord is, there is liberty" (2 Cor. 3:17). The Spirit of the Lord in you wants to liberate

you. Cooperate with the grace of God and let Him accelerate the renewal of your mind.

Once you see the lie, repent for agreeing with it. Break all agreement with the lie. Renounce it, in Jesus' name. Meditate on the truth that combats the lie. Remember, "Jesus said to the people who believed in him, 'You are truly my disciples if you remain faithful to my teachings. And you will know the truth, and the truth will set you free'" (John 8:31-32 NLT). And again, "Therefore if the Son makes you free, you shall be free indeed" (John 8:36). Once you break free, be sure to "Stand fast therefore in the liberty by which Christ has made us free, and do not be entangled again with a yoke of bondage" (Gal. 5:1).

## FASTING CAN HELP RENEW YOUR MIND

One last thought: fasting can help. Fasting is abstaining from food or some activity to focus on God. But it's just as much what you do instead of eating as it is the fast itself. If you fast and sit on the couch and watch TV all day, you are going on a glorified diet. You will get some of the benefits of fasting, but you are missing the spiritual point. Fasting is not a diet. It's a spiritual discipline.

Andrew Murray wrote, "Prayer is the reaching out after God and the unseen; fasting, the letting go of all that is of the seen and temporal. ...Fasting helps to express, to deepen, and to confirm the resolution that we are ready to sacrifice anything, to sacrifice ourselves, to attain what we seek for the kingdom of God."[2]

Fasting can help us hear more clearly from God. Fasting can help detoxify your body. Fasting helps cleanse your soul of toxic emotions and bring deliverance. Remember, Jesus spoke of fasting in the context of deliverance: "This kind can come out by nothing but prayer and fasting" (Mark 9:29). But even from a scientific perspective, fasting helps your mental health.

Fasting interventions have shown effectiveness in alleviating stress, anxiety, and depressive symptoms, according to the National Institute of Heath's (NIH) National Library of medicine. Dr. Dan Brennan spoke about the psychological benefits of fasting, including mental function and increased willpower. "When you fast, your body has less toxic materials flowing through the blood and lymphatic system, making it easier for you to think," he wrote. "While fasting, the energy you'd normally use to digest food is available to be used by the brain."[3] If you need a soul detox, try fasting.

## NOTES

1.  Jennifer LeClaire, *101 Tactics for Spiritual Warfare* (Lake Mary, FL: Charisma House, 2018), 19.

2.  Andrew Murray, *With Christ in the School of Prayer* (New York, NY: Fleming H. Revell Company, 1885), https://ccel.org/ccel/murray/prayer/prayer.XIII.html ;accessed March 23, 2023.

3.  Dan Brennan, MD, "Psychological Benefits of Fasting," WebMD, Benefits of Fasting, October 25, 2021, https://www.webmd.com/diet/psychological-benefits-of-fasting; accessed March 23, 2023.

# CHAPTER 11

# CULTIVATING THE OIL
# OF INTIMACY

After eight years in an increasingly toxic prophetic church, I was dried out and burned out. Actually, that's an understatement. I was emotionally, physically and spiritually exhausted. That's also probably an understatement. I never wanted to step foot back in a church. I just wanted to sleep. I suppose I felt like Elijah after the showdown at Mount Carmel.

That's high-level prophetic witchcraft indeed. And when I left that church I was completely torn down. I would lie in bed on Sunday mornings feeling like I had been run over by a truck. At first, I couldn't even think about trying to go to another church. Eventually, I found a church that met on Friday nights only and it seemed perfect because I sincerely needed a break from what I came to know as Sunday morning church as usual. I thought things would calm down and that the church I left would stop harassing me.

What I didn't know is the warfare against me would get worse instead of better. But because I cultivated the oil of intimacy, I was able to withstand the emotional terrorism and psychological warfare. Because I cultivated the oil of intimacy, His voice was the loudest I heard. Because I cultivated the oil of intimacy, the curse did not land and I was blessed beyond measure instead. What the enemy meant for harm, God turned for good (see Gen. 50:20).

I started cultivating this oil accidentally. See, in the toxic church I left there was no mention of intimacy. There was no talk of God's love—other than to convince us His love was conditional upon our behavior, which is heresy. There was mostly talk of spiritual warfare, Jezebel, and the believer's authority and the Kingdom of God. It was unbalanced at best. Although I learned how to fight, I didn't learn to love.

A friend of mine who had previously left the church suggested that I start listening to a 24/7 worship livestream from International House of Prayer in Kansas City. I went to sleep listening to love songs to Jesus. Little did I know, the worship was renewing my mind, breaking off wrong teaching that was hindering my ability to receive God's love, and more. Eventually, I found the balance of standing as a warrior and sitting at His feet as a worshiper. It took time, but I cultivated the oil of intimacy.

## I WAS BURNED OUT AND STRESSED OUT

Cultivating the oil of intimacy is critical, even if you are not burned out and stressed out. Let me put it another way. If you don't cultivate the oil of intimacy, you will eventually find yourself burned

out and stressed out even if you aren't trying to escape prophetic witchcraft.

Jesus told a parable about wise and foolish virgins that highlights the dire need of every believer to cultivate the oil of intimacy. We would do well to meditate on this and extract from it every lesson we can. We find the parable in Matthew 25:1-12:

> *Then the kingdom of heaven shall be likened to ten virgins who took their lamps and went out to meet the bridegroom. Now five of them were wise, and five were foolish. Those who were foolish took their lamps and took no oil with them, but the wise took oil in their vessels with their lamps. But while the bridegroom was delayed, they all slumbered and slept.*
>
> *And at midnight a cry was heard: "Behold, the bridegroom is coming; go out to meet him!" Then all those virgins arose and trimmed their lamps. And the foolish said to the wise, "Give us some of your oil, for our lamps are going out." But the wise answered, saying, "No, lest there should not be enough for us and you; but go rather to those who sell, and buy for yourselves." And while they went to buy, the bridegroom came, and those who were ready went in with him to the wedding; and the door was shut.*
>
> *Afterward the other virgins came also, saying, "Lord, Lord, open to us!" But he answered and said, "Assuredly, I say to you, I do not know you."*

## I NEEDED AN OIL CHANGE

When I was bound by prophetic witchcraft, I was like the foolish virgin who worked, worked, and worked more for approval and blessings. I didn't understand who I really was, and ministry became an idol. I was running on fumes instead of oil, burned out and stressed out and driven to do more and more. Prophetic witchcraft led me to work for Him but not with Him and, as it turns out, I was not building the Kingdom of God. I was building a man's kingdom. Of course, I didn't know it.

What I needed was an oil change. I learned this in the natural the hard way. When I was in college, I had a little silver Toyota. I liked the car but I didn't take care of it well. My grandfather was always asking me if I got the oil changed. I thought he was just nagging me and blew him off. That was foolishness! Once day, seemingly out of nowhere, my car broke down on the side of the road.

I didn't realize it, but not changing the oil had warped the engine components. I didn't notice it, but my engine was not running efficiently for a long while. Then, suddenly, I experienced complete engine failure. That's what happens in our souls when we don't get fresh oil. In my case, my oil was defiled with prophetic witchcraft. There was little intimacy to speak of. The wrong kind of oil was going into my engine, so to speak. The results were devastating.

Although I had a personal relationship with Jesus and spent time with Him every day, I was working for Him without grace. I needed a "come to Jesus moment." Jesus said in Matthew 11:28-31, "Come to Me, all you who labor and are heavy laden, and I will give you rest. Take My yoke upon you and learn from Me, for I am gentle and lowly in heart, and you will find rest for your souls. For My yoke is easy and My burden is light."

See, I wasn't under Christ's yoke. I was under the yoke of prophetic witchcraft. I didn't feel God's pleasure in the work. I felt driven instead of led, and it seemed nothing I ever did was good enough. I wasn't making the oil my first priority. I was like the Galatians Paul exhorted and corrected in Galatians 5:1, "Stand fast therefore in the liberty by which Christ has made us free, and do not be entangled again with a yoke of bondage."

## PROPHETIC WITCHCRAFT'S GUILT AND CONDEMNATION

Prophetic witchcraft will heap guilt and condemnation on you so you don't want to spend time with God. You may not realize you are riddled with guilt and condemnation—and perhaps you are not. But if you have submitted to leadership that operates prophetic witchcraft, chances are guilt and condemnation are keeping you from pressing into intimacy with God.

The definition of *guilt* is "the fact of having committed a breach of conduct, especially violating the law and involving a penalty," according to *Merriam-Webster*'s dictionary. Noteworthy is the reality that you can carry guilt whether or not you are actually guilty of anything. That's called false guilt. False guilt comes from the enemy's lies through people or vain imaginations (see 2 Cor. 10:5). Remember, one name of the enemy is the Accuser of the brethren. He accuses us day and night (see Rev. 12:10).

The enemy's guilt produces death. Paul wrote, "For godly sorrow produces repentance leading to salvation, not to be regretted; but the sorrow of the world produces death" (2 Cor. 7:10). Guilt can make you paranoid. Guilt can sabotage your success. Guilt can make you defensive over constructive criticism. Guilt can make you apologize for things you didn't do.

Remember, the definition of *guilt* is "the fact of having committed a breach of conduct, especially violating the law and involving a penalty." One of the penalties of guilt that the enemy lays on you in the spirit realm is a feeling of condemnation. One definition of *condemned* is "declared to be reprehensible, wrong or evil."

When you have a condemnation mindset, you feel you are a bad person. You feel you've done something so bad you can't be forgiven. You feel like you deserve bad things. You won't forgive yourself. Thank God for the words the Holy Spirit inspired Paul to write in Romans 8:1: "There is therefore now no condemnation to those who are in Christ Jesus, who do not walk according to the flesh, but according to the Spirit."

Another definition of *condemned* is "pronounced guilty and sentenced to punishment, especially death." When you are walking in condemnation, you are not living the abundant life Jesus died to give you (see John 10:10). You are walking under a cloud of death. Condemnation clouds your perception of God's goodness. Condemnation affects your intercession, your relationships, and just about everything else in your life. Condemnation doesn't lead people to repentance. It's the kindness of God that leads people to repentance (see Rom. 2:4). I like The Passion Translation of Romans 8:1: "So now the case is closed. There remains no accusing voice of condemnation against those who are joined in life-union with Jesus, the Anointed One."

Another definition of *condemned* is "officially declared unfit for use." When you are walking with the death cloud of condemnation over you, you feel like God can't use you. You feel that you are not worthy to do anything for God. That's just what the enemy wants you to believe! He wants to keep you in the cave of condemnation so that you don't fulfill your destiny.

Look at *The Message* version of Romans 8:1:

> *With the arrival of Jesus, the Messiah, that fateful dilemma is resolved. Those who enter into Christ's being-here-for-us no longer have to live under a continuous, low-lying black cloud. A new power is in operation. The Spirit of life in Christ, like a strong wind, has magnificently cleared the air, freeing you from a fated lifetime of brutal tyranny at the hands of sin and death.*

Jesus didn't even condemn the woman caught in the act of adultery! She was absolutely guilty and deserving of death according to the Jewish law, but He did not condemn her. The religious system wanted her dead, but Jesus released her from the condemnation and admonished her not to sin anymore.

Many years ago, the Lord asked me if I could tell Him what the difference was between the Holy Spirit's conviction and the enemy's condemnation. I guess I didn't know the answer or He wouldn't have asked me. So I asked Him, "What is the difference, Lord?" His reply? "The difference is love." Even the very definitions of these two words are different. Condemnation is a damnable sentence. Conviction is defined as the state of being convinced of error or compelled to admit the truth. But here's the thing. If you don't know the love of God, it feels like condemnation to you.

## CHECK YOUR HEART

When you hear the voice of guilt and condemnation, check your heart. Is this the enemy speaking to you, or are you condemning yourself? If you are hearing this voice from the outside, you need to cast it down. Cast down the imagination (see 2 Cor. 10:5). If you are hearing the voice from inside, if you are condemning yourself, you need to forgive yourself. Consider 1 John 3:20 AMPC:

> *Whenever our hearts in [tormenting] self-accusation make us feel guilty and condemn us. [For we are in God's hands.] For He is above and greater than our consciences (our hearts), and He knows (perceives and understands) everything [nothing is hidden from Him].*

The Passion Translation puts it this way:

> *Whenever our hearts make us feel guilty and remind us of our failures, we know that God is much greater and more merciful than our conscience, and he knows everything there is to know about us. My delightfully loved*

*friends, when our hearts don't condemn us, we have a*
*bold freedom to speak face-to-face with God.*

When we feel guilt and condemnation because of something we've done, we need to do what 1 John 1:9 and Hebrews 4:16 says, "Let us therefore come boldly to the throne of grace, that we may obtain mercy and find grace to help in time of need." And 1 John 1:9 exhorts, "If we confess our sins, He is faithful and just to forgive us our sins and to cleanse us from all unrighteousness." Then let it go.

## UNDERSTANDING CHRIST'S PASSION FOR YOU

When you understand the passion of Christ for you, you will pursue an intimate relationship with Him. I wasn't taught about the unconditional love of God. I was taught the love of God was conditional upon performance. I had to renew my mind to the love and passion of Jesus for me—a passion that made Him willing to die on a bloody cross for me and that spurs Him to continue making intercession for me even now (see Rom. 8:34).

I had to meditate on verses like 1 John 3:1, "Behold what manner of love the Father has bestowed on us, that we should be called children of God!" And 1 John 4:10, "In this is love, not that we loved God, but that He loved us and sent His Son to be the propitiation for our sins." And 1 John 4:19, "We love Him because He first loved us."

I kept meditating on verses like Romans 5:8, which assures, "But God demonstrates His own love toward us, in that while we were still sinners, Christ died for us." And Romans 8:38-39, "For I am persuaded that neither death nor life, nor angels nor principalities nor powers, nor things present nor things to come, nor height nor depth, nor any other created thing, shall be able to separate us from the love of God which is in Christ Jesus our Lord."

These and other verses stirred in me a passion for the One who has passion for me. Meditating on these Scriptures helped me understand I didn't have to perform for His love—that He not only loves me but actually likes me. Ephesians 1:6 tells us we are accepted in Christ. We must continually renew our mind to these realities. When we do, we will be a person of one thing, like David, who cried out, "One thing I have desired of the Lord, that will I seek: That I may dwell in the house of the Lord all the days of my life, to behold the beauty of the Lord, and to inquire in His temple" (Ps. 27:4).

## CULTIVATING INTIMACY WITH GOD

How do you create intimacy with God? There's no single answer. It's a life of immersion, walking in the Spirit, talking to the Spirit, fellowshipping with the Spirit, praying in the Spirit. Remember, the Holy Spirit is the Spirit of Holy. Start by consecrating yourself to Him. Consecration is pulling away from something to draw near to something—or in this case, Someone. Consider fasting—if not food, the entertainment or media—to spend more time with Him. Hebrews 12:14 tells us, "Pursue peace with all people, and holiness, without which no one will see the Lord."

Invest your time in Him. Make an appointment with God every day in your personal prayer closet and keep that appointment. As you read—and meditate—on the Word, seek to understand what He likes and what He doesn't like. Pursue a knowledge of God and His ways. Study His character and His attributes. Look at the operations of the Holy Spirit in the Old Testament and New Testament. Check out my course "Walking in the Spirit" at www .schoolofthespirit.tv for an in-depth study.

Ask God for the gift of hunger, which David possessed. In Psalm 63:1-5 he wrote:

> *O God, You are my God; early will I seek You; my soul thirsts for You; my flesh longs for You in a dry and thirsty land where there is no water. So I have looked for You in the sanctuary, to see Your power and Your glory. Because Your lovingkindness is better than life, my lips shall praise You. Thus I will bless You while I live; I will lift up my hands in Your name. My soul shall be satisfied as with marrow and fatness, and my mouth shall praise You with joyful lips.*

Dialogue with the Holy Spirit. Talk to Him throughout the day. Thank Him for His help. Ask Him for wisdom. Praise and worship Him. Present your body as a living sacrifice (see Rom. 12:1-2). Crucify your flesh. Glorify God in your body. Set your heart to do His will and be quick to repent when you miss the mark. Ask God for a greater sensitivity to His heart. Lean in to abide in Him. Surrender to Him moment by moment. It's a lifelong pursuit—and eternal pursuit—but it's worth it. The closer you are to God, the less likely you are to fall into prophetic witchcraft's snare again. He'll heal you, deliver you, and restore you for His glory.

# CHAPTER 12

# DELIVERANCE FROM THE VICTIM
# MENTALITY

After I suffered at the hand of prophetic witchcraft, I developed a victim mentality. When I left the abusive church, I gave up my front-row seats. I lost every friend I had. I lost every teaching opportunity I had and more. I lost a lot. When we lose, we grieve. But if we don't grieve in a healthy way we can end up feeling like victims.

I still remember when the Holy Spirit confronted me on this mindset. I was shocked. I didn't want to admit that I had a victim mentality. Don't get me wrong. I was a victim of prophetic witchcraft. I was a victim of apostolic abuse. I was an innocent victim. I suffered evil at the hands of others. But it was my choice to develop a victim mentality.

Too many people who are victims of prophetic witchcraft adopt a victim mentality. A victim mentality is the mindset that you are a victim. Keep this in mind: you aren't born with a victim mentality.

You develop this mindset through injustices, tragedy, or abuses, such as prophetic witchcraft. There was a trigger event that started the cycle.

You may think, "I don't have a victim mentality." You may not, but don't brush off the possibility. The victim mentality is sometimes subtle, but there are signs that the voice of victimhood is renewing your mind. The good news is, there is grace to break free from the victim mentality. But first you need to see it for what it is. As I always say, an enemy exposed is an enemy defeated.

## SIGNS YOU HAVE A VICTIM MENTALITY

It's up to you whether you adopt a victim or a victor mentality. But I urge you not to give the enemy the satisfaction of further victimizing you through this mindset. A victim mentality leaves us with a distorted view of reality. We see everything through victim-colored glasses and develop distrust for people who we haven't even gotten to know. A victim mentality steals our joy, damages our relationships, and makes us paranoid.

A victim mentality manifests as a feeling of powerlessness to fix the problems in your life or even cope with them. You may magnify the devil's attack and exalt his power over God's power. You may concentrate on what the devil has done or is doing to the point that you're giving glory to the enemy's work instead of magnifying the Lord.

This is a dangerous trap. David said in Psalm 34:3-4, "Oh, magnify the Lord with me, and let us exalt His name together. I sought the Lord, and He heard me, and delivered me from all my fears."

*Magnify* means "to increase in significance" or "to enlarge in fact or opinions." When we magnify the devil's facts over God's truth, we feel like victims. But when we cry out to God, He will deliver us from the victim mentality driven by the pain prophetic witchcraft inflicted upon our soul.

When you have a victim mentality, you may think people are out to get you. At its extreme, you become paranoid and unable to enter trusting relationships with leaders—or just anybody, really. You may even wonder sometimes if God is on your side. Let me set the record straight. God is always for you and stands against prophetic witchcraft. And Romans 8:31 assures is, "If God is for us, who can be against us?"

When you have a victim mentality, you get easily offended when someone tries to help you see your life from God's perspective. You may also reject godly counsel because you feel like no one could possibly understand. You try to justify your victim mentality because what you dealt with was so bad nobody could relate unless they went through the same thing. But Jesus gets it. Jesus is a High Priest who is able to sympathize with us because He was tempted in the same ways we are without sinning (see Heb. 4:15).

When you have a victim mentality, you may refuse to take any responsibility for your position in life. You won't take responsibility for falling for the prophetic witchcraft. You don't consider that you could be responding wrong to the circumstances in which you find yourself. You blame the devil, other people, and even God but don't look at how you could change your perspective. Let me say this clearly, "Life is not fair, but God is just." Be willing to examine your heart. Lamentations 3:40 admonishes: "Let us search out and examine our ways, and turn back to the Lord."

When you have a victim mentality, you get upset when people don't give you the sympathy you think you deserve. When they don't RSVP to your pity party, you feel rejected. The only ones who join in your pity party are other miserable people who want to take turns with you complaining about their lives. You may even host your own private pity parties. You feel sorry for yourself. Self-pity attracts devils. The devil always shows up at your pity party to agree with the voice of pity in your life. Misery loves company.

When you have a victim mentality, you walk in a state of fear, doubt, and negativity about your circumstances. "I can't" is common in your vocabulary. You may feel at some level you deserve what you are getting. You feel like you have the right to complain because of what has happened to you. But Jesus never complained even when He hung on a cross. And victims want vengeance. But vengeance is not yours to take. Paul wrote, "Beloved, do not avenge yourselves, but rather give place to wrath; for it is written, 'Vengeance is Mine, I will repay,' says the Lord" (Rom. 12:19).

Even though something devastating has happened to you, God doesn't see you as a victim. He sees you as more than a conqueror in Christ (see Rom. 8:37). And beyond what I shared so far, He has a lot of advice on how to deal with a victim mentality.

## DO YOU WANT TO GET WELL?

Jesus ran into a man with a victim mentality, and the encounter offers some insight into the stumbling blocks to deliverance as well as some keys to freedom. We see the story after Jesus went up to Jerusalem to the feast of the Jews. By the sheep gate there was a pool with five porticoes called Bethesda. I stood there when I was in Israel imagining the scene, which we find in John 5:

> *In these lay a great multitude of sick people, blind, lame, paralyzed, waiting for the moving of the water. For an angel went down at a certain time into the pool and stirred up the water; then whoever stepped in first, after the stirring of the water, was made well of whatever disease he had* (John 5:3-4).

Consider the scene. There was a great multitude. There's a great multitude in the Body of Christ who need deliverance from prophetic witchcraft. I get testimonies all over the world from people who lost everything they had because of prophetic witchcraft. Some have even had a crisis of faith because of prophetic witchcraft. This multitude was waiting for a miracle. The story continues:

> *Now a certain man was there who had an infirmity thirty-eight years. When Jesus saw him lying there, and knew that he already had been in that condition a long time, He said to him, "Do you want to be made well?"* (John 5:5-6)

Catch that. This man was sick for thirty-eight years. Some people who suffer fallout from prophetic witchcraft stay in bondage for decades. Some won't step foot back in the church because of what happened to them. This is a mistake, as we often find healing and deliverance in the context of community—not a community of other sick people but a community of faith. This man was hanging out with sick people for decades. I can imagine the victim mentality permeated the porticoes.

Jesus asked the man a question: "Do you want to be made well?" On the surface, that seems like a ridiculous question. Of course he wants to get healed. Of course you want to get healed. When Jesus asks us a question, it's not because He doesn't know the answer. Our answer becomes a prayer request that brings the freedom we desire. It also, at times, causes us to search our soul and confront obstacles to our healing or deliverance. Sometimes we need to go through inner healing, which requires some hard work on our part.

In John 5:7, you can see the crippled man's victim mentality when He answers Jesus' question. I always imagine him saying this in a whiney voice: "Sir, I have no man to put me into the pool when the water is stirred up; but while I am coming, another steps down before me." Can you see it? When Jesus asked the man if he wanted to get well, he should have said, "Yes, Lord." Or he could have at least said, "I believe. Help my unbelief." But he felt like a victim because no one would help him.

Think about it for a minute. Here was this man, sitting on the edge of a supernatural deliverance, and he couldn't see the opportunity. He only saw the challenge. The Son of God was standing right in front of him, ready to help him, and his victim mentality caused him to focus on the problem rather than the solution.

Here was this man making excuses to Jesus about why he couldn't get healed. He had wrapped up his identity in his obstacles, trials, and warfare. I tell you the truth, I would have scooted myself to the edge of the pool in thirty-eight years. I would have devised a plan or paid someone to roll me over into the pool when the angel came to trouble the water. But a victim mentality paralyzed his mind in the same way a sickness paralyzed his body.

Notice what happened next. Jesus didn't show him any pity. But He did show him compassion. Watch what happened next: "Jesus said to him, 'Rise, take up your bed and walk.' And immediately the man was made well, took up his bed, and walked" (John 5:8-9). That's how fast his deliverance happened. Immediately. That's how fast your deliverance from prophetic witchcraft can be. Sometimes, you need someone to confront your victim mentality like I just did.

## CHOOSE A VICTORY MINDSET

You can choose a victory mindset. You can choose to walk as more than a conqueror in Christ. You can choose to renew your mind with the Word of the God of your victory. You can break the powers of the victim spirit off your mind and find deliverance for your soul.

Meditate on 1 Corinthians 15:57, "But thanks be to God, who gives us the victory through our Lord Jesus Christ." Meditate on Romans 8:37, "Yet in all these things we are more than conquerors through Him who loved us." Meditate on 2 Corinthians 2:14, "Now thanks be to God who always leads us in triumph in Christ, and through us diffuses the fragrance of His knowledge in every place." Meditate on 1 John 5:4, "For whatever is born of God overcomes the world. And this is the victory that has overcome the world— our faith." Meditate on Revelation 12:11, "And they overcame him by the blood of the Lamb and by the word of their testimony, and they did not love their lives to the death."

I heard the Lord say:

*"You are not a victim. You are a victor. And even though the enemy has victimized you, even though the enemy has terrorized you, even though the enemy has even made you feel at times like you are losing your mind, there is pay-back and there is sevenfold return and even more so as you follow Me. I won't just give you double for your trouble; I won't just give you triple for your trial, but I will give you sevenfold as a minimum return on the investment that you made in trying to do My will and not understanding fully yet how to fight the wicked one."*

Pray this prayer:

*Father, in the name of Jesus, I repent of taking on a victim mindset when Your Word tells me I am victorious in Christ. Forgive me for allowing the enemy a place in my mind, will, and emotions. I renounce the spirit of victim. I renounce all victimhood and victim mindsets. I command the spirit of victim to loose my mind, in the name of Jesus. I declare I am more than a conqueror in Christ.*

# CHAPTER 13

# REBUILDING TRUST IN THE
# PROPHETIC

**W**hen I left an abusive apostolic church, I wasn't just hurt by the apostolic. I was hurt by the prophetic. Deeply hurt. Beyond the apostle cursing me and the pastor trying to crush my spirit, my mentor used her prophetic gifting to shame me, accuse me, and abuse me. It was beyond heartbreaking.

The prophetic witchcraft came at me in waves. I was publicly humiliated. I was privately slandered in the name of prophecy. Almost overnight, I was suddenly demonized. I was accused of operating in a cadre of spirits even though I had been up front, leading, and teaching from the platform for years with no correction until I refused to continue to let them be my puppeteer.

After I left, the apostle announced from the platform that Jezebel took me out and started making videos on how prophets fail and how Jezebel woos prophets. As I mentioned before, he actually stood up in Sunday service some weeks after I left sharing through false tears that I had turned my back on Christ. It was his way to cover up what he was afraid would be his own exposure.

What the apostle said couldn't have been further from the truth. I didn't run from Christ. I ran toward Christ, the Healer, to bind up my broken heart. I ran toward Christ, the Liberator, to find deliverance from prophetic witchcraft. Through that year or so, I grieved. I sometimes wondered if I should have stayed on and tried to pray them through it. And I had difficulty trusting apostolic and prophetic leaders again.

In fact, even after I went through a yearlong process of healing, deliverance, and restoration from prophetic witchcraft, I still got nervous when a leader wanted to talk to me. I always thought I was in trouble. I was afraid that I was going to meet with more prophetic witchcraft. In honesty, it took me several more years to shake that off—partly because of other run-ins with leaders operating in prophetic witchcraft along the way.

I won't go into all those stories here. I will say this, though—after you break loose from prophetic witchcraft you may again encounter others operating in the same deceptive practices. You may even get burned again. It will bring up memories of the original incidents. It will feel familiar and may be painful. Don't stay there. When you encounter prophetic witchcraft after your deliverance, it's just the enemy trying to put you in another form of bondage called bitterness.

# IDENTIFICATIONAL REPENTANCE FOR THE PROPHETIC MOVEMENT

I believe in the true prophetic ministry with every fiber of my being. It is a vital ministry in the Body of Christ that has seen many come into salvation, deliverance, emotional and physical healing, and many other blessings. Christ gave prophets to the church (see Eph. 4:11). We cannot discredit the entire movement over the growing number of false prophets.

I probably don't know you or have done anything to hurt you, but as a leader in the modern-day prophetic movement I want to take a moment to identificationally repent on behalf of the prophets who burned you, cursed you, used you, robbed you, and otherwise abused you (see Dan. 9:1-19; Neh. 1:4-7). I want to ask for your forgiveness for the prophetic witchcraft you experienced. I am so sorry for what happened to you.

What is identificational repentance? Identificational repentance is when one person repents for corporate sin in a people group. There are plenty of examples in the Old Testament, from Moses repenting for the complaining Israelites (see Exod. 34:8-9) to Daniel repenting on behalf of Israel (see Dan. 9:20).

With that, I repent to you on behalf of those in the prophetic movement whose ill motives harmed you. I repent for the lack of accountability. I repent for the lack of discernment, for the lack of true mothering and fathering of the next generation, for caving in to the pressure to prophesy, for prophesying along political party lines, for the lack of humility, for promoting people too fast in an age of social media, for exalting gifting over character, for not learning from past mistakes in the prophetic movement, for prophesying with wrong motives, for not confronting prophetic witchcraft, for selling prophecy, for engendering an overdependence on prophets instead of equipping the Body to hear His voice for themselves, and for other grievances. I repent on behalf of those in the prophetic movement who committed spiritual crimes against you and ask for forgiveness. I hope you can find it in your heart to forgive them.

## TAP INTO THE POWER OF FORGIVENESS

Will you forgive? The one who took you captive through prophetic witchcraft may never ask your forgiveness. They may never repent. They may have a reprobate mind (see Rom. 1:28). They may be completely deceived. Their conscious may have been seared with a hot iron (see 1 Tim. 4:2). But that doesn't mean you shouldn't forgive. Forgiveness is part and parcel of getting free and staying free—and being part of the solution.

Forgiveness is part of rebuilding trust in the prophetic. Distrust will seep into every area of your life if you don't forgive as Christ commands. In Mark 11:25, Christ exhorts, "And whenever you stand praying, if you have anything against anyone, forgive him, that your Father in heaven may also forgive you your trespasses." And in Matthew 6:14-15, He admonishes, "For if you forgive men their trespasses, your heavenly Father will also forgive you. But if you do not forgive men their trespasses, neither will your Father forgive your trespasses." And Paul wrote, "Even as Christ forgave you, so you also must do" (Col. 3:13).

Unforgiveness is like taking poison and hoping your enemy will die. Ask yourself this question: what if the Lord forgave you in the same proportion that you forgave the people who hurt you? Would you feel comfortable with that? In Matthew 5:44-45, Jesus tells us, "But I say to you, love your enemies, bless those who curse you, do good to those who hate you, and pray for those who spitefully use you and persecute you, that you may be sons of your Father in heaven."

## REJECT OVERDEPENDENCE ON PROPHETS

If we've been burned in the prophetic, it may be that we put too much trust in the prophet rather than seeking the Lord for ourselves. As I've said many, many times over the years, too many Christians are too dependent on prophets to tell them what God is saying. We need to look in the mirror and take responsibility for our part in the pain.

Don't get me wrong. I am not against personal prophecy. I prophesy over people at the Awakening House of Prayer and various conferences all the time. But as I've said many times, prophetic ministry doesn't operate like a gumball machine. You can't put in a quarter—or send an email or Facebook message—and out comes a prophetic word. It just doesn't work that way. There's a ton of pressure on prophets to have a word on demand. This is how some prophets wind up operating in prophetic witchcraft.

We need to return to the foundations. Every believer has the capacity to hear from God. Jesus said His sheep know His voice (see John 10:27). But many believers do not discern the voice of the Lord, which is one reason there is an unhealthy dependence on prophets.

Indeed, many treat prophets like psychics. Many believers put unhealthy pressure on prophetic people to "gimme a word" or get sucked into pay-for-prophecy scams on the Internet that I've pointed out in this series of books. Every day I get at least a handful of digital requests from precious people all over the world desperately seeking a prophetic word. As I've said before, some come begging. Others come demanding. Still others come with money in hand to buy a prophecy or dream interpretation.

True prophets don't work to make you dependent on their gift to guide you. Phony prophets specialize in this area. True prophets live by the Ephesians 4:11 model: to equip the saints for the work of the ministry. Phony prophets specialize in clever marketing schemes to put a quick buck in their pocket in exchange for a prophetic word that may of come from their spirit—or a familiar spirit—but isn't likely to have originated with the Spirit of God.

When I get phone calls, emails, and Facebook messages begging, demanding, and offering to pay for prophetic words, it grieves me because I can see clearly that there is still a major misunderstanding about prophetic ministry in the Body of Christ. And that can put these precious believers in danger of getting merchandised, deceived, and otherwise steered in the wrong direction in the name of sincerely "seeking God." I don't have time to respond to each and every one in detail about the role of the prophet, why it's inappropriate for prophets to charge for prophecies, or how to hear from God.

But let me assure you of this: God wants to speak to you. In fact, He's probably speaking to you more than you realize. Precious saints, God wants to speak to you directly. Don't run to a prophet—and don't pay a prophet—for prophetic words. Run to God and sow your time into fellowshipping with the Holy Spirit. You won't be disappointed and you won't walk away with a manufactured poor prophecy that leads you in the wrong direction. The Holy Spirit will lead you and guide you into all truth (see John 16:13). That's a promise from King Jesus. Amen.

## DON'T ASSUME ALL PROPHETS ARE SHADY

Don't throw the baby out with the bathwater. Many people who fall under the spell or are attacked by prophetic witchcraft become sour about the whole prophetic movement. Yes, there are many false prophets and many manipulative prophets, but that is no reason to throw the baby out with the bathwater.

We must not abandon or discredit prophetic ministry altogether just because prophetic witchcraft has infiltrated some camps or because false prophets are rising, as Jesus said they would. We shouldn't be surprised. Rather, we must hold fast to the truth and embrace the ministry of true prophets who are committed to delivering the unadulterated prophetic word of God and equipping believers to discern God's voice, know His will, and see what the Father is doing. Suspicion will block your discernment.

## LEARN TO TRUST YOURSELF

You may be ashamed that you fell for prophetic witchcraft. You may not trust yourself to judge between good and evil. That's understandable after what you've experienced, but don't let the devil shame and condemn you. Determine why you fell into prophetic witchcraft's net and determine to repent and renew your mind.

Chances are, you had a check in your spirit before you fell into that pit and ignored it for whatever reason. Or maybe you haven't developed enough sensitivity to the Holy Spirit to discern His leadership. It happens to everyone. Get equipped. Read the whole trilogy of this series, which includes *Discerning Prophetic Witchcraft* and *Exposing Prophetic Witchcraft*. God will teach you to navigate the realms of true and false.

## TRUSTING GOD ABOVE ALL

Ultimately, we must put our trust in God. He rescued you out of the pit of prophetic witchcraft, whether in your ignorance or in your disobedience. He will help you discern prophetic witchcraft in the future. Now, you have some experience so it will be easier to discern. The Holy Spirit will help you test the spirits to see if it's true or false. He will help you.

And remember, Romans 8:28 is still true: "And we know that all things work together for good to those who love God, to those who are the called according to His purpose." God will give you beauty for ashes. He will give you the oil of joy for mourning. He will make the crooked places straight and the wrong things right. He will level the mountains and break through gates of bronze. He will restore the years the locust worm ate. He will bring justice and He will vindicate. Trust in the Lord and do good.

# ABOUT
## JENNIFER LECLAIRE

Jennifer LeClaire is senior leader of Awakening House of Prayer in Fort Lauderdale, Florida, founder of the Ignite Network, and founder of the Awakening Prayer Hubs prayer movement. Jennifer formerly served as the first-ever female editor of *Charisma* magazine and is a prolific author of over 50 books. You can find Jennifer online or shoot her an email at info@jenniferleclaire.org.

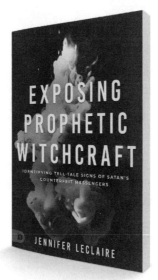

From

# Jennifer LeClaire

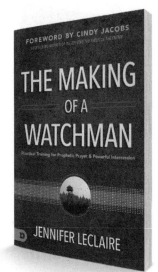

## The "Watchman Anointing" is being released in this hour!

If you seek to better understand the times and seasons, read on. If you are compelled by Jesus' words to watch and to pray, this book is for you!

Throughout Scripture, God appointed His watchmen to guard and protect Israel. The watchman's duty was to warn of coming danger, calling God's people to follow the Lord's ways. A watchman's ministry offered both warning and hope. Though they were often not well received, their message and ministry were critical. It is no different today.

In *The Making of a Watchman*, veteran prophet and seer, Jennifer LeClaire draws from scriptural examples and personal experience, revealing how to operate in this crucial ministry – not only to anticipate the enemy's schemes, but to align with God's Kingdom plans and purposes.

God still appoints His watchmen over cities and nations – those who will proclaim His Kingdom and offer hope in the midst of chaos. Are you called to this office? Come along with Jennifer LeClaire and learn to respond with Kingdom perspective to the changing times and seasons!

## Purchase your copy wherever books are sold

From
# Jennifer LeClaire

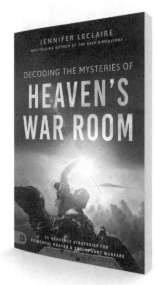

## A Heavenly Revelation of Spiritual Warfare Secrets

Jennifer LeClaire, globally recognized prophet, spiritual warfare trainer, and prayer leader, received a vivid, visionary encounter in the War Room of Heaven.

*In this vision, I saw a veil rip open from the top to bottom. As I peered behind the veil, I saw a long walkway with bookshelves on either side. I suddenly had a knowing in my spirit that these books were full of mysteries that became revelations to generations past—revelations recorded and lost.*

Through *Decoding the Mysteries of Heaven's War Room* Jennifer shares powerful, Bible-based revelations that will empower you to partner with God's purposes, and achieve greater victory in your life!

Over the course of 21 vivid and revelatory Heavenly encounters, your understanding of prayer and spiritual warfare will be forever transformed.

Learn how to partner with the War Room of Heaven to pray prayers that secure victory on Earth. The Mysteries of the Kingdom are yours to discover and walk in!

## Purchase your copy wherever books are sold

From

# Jennifer LeClaire

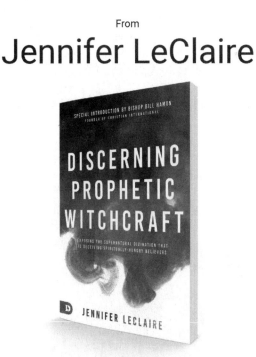

## Your Holy Spirit Handbook to
## Surviving Last Days Deception.

*On that day many will say to me, Lord, Lord, did we not prophesy in your name, and cast out demons in your name, and do many mighty works in your name? - Matthew 7:22*

**Are they prophesying by the Holy Spirit... or ministering under a demonic influence?**

Jennifer LeClaire received a startling prophetic word that a showdown was coming to the body of Christwhere both true and false prophets will be exposed. In this book she presents a confrontational yet constructive word of warning to the contemporary Spirit-empowered movement. More than ever, there is a great need in the modern prophetic community to be discerning of what is true and what is false.

When you learn to recognize and resist satans counterfeits, you will build your life upon unshakeable Truth and thrive in victory during days of darkness and compromise.

## Purchase your copy wherever books are sold

From

# Jennifer LeClaire

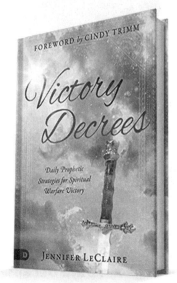

### Declarations and decrees that give
### you an advantage over the enemy!

The enemy of every believer prowls around like a roaring lion, searching for lives to devour. But when you are equipped with Biblical warfare strategies, you have the authority to declare, "Not today, satan!"

Bestselling author and veteran spiritual warrior, Jennifer Le-Claire offers *Victory Decrees*—a daily devotional of prophetic warfare strategies that will empower you towards victory!

Begin every day positioned for triumph!

### Purchase your copy wherever books are sold

From

# Jennifer LeClaire

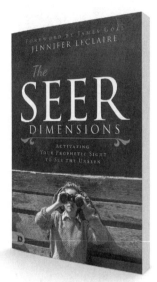

The seer realm lies just beyond what your natural eyes can see. This dimension is full of activity, both angelic and demonic. *The Seer Dimensions* offers revelation and practical teaching that will help you understand and navigate the heights and depths of the spiritual world.

Many people who see in the spirit often don't know what they are seeing, or understand the dimensions of spiritual sight. But this landmark book will help you unlock these mysteries!

Best selling author, Jennifer LeClaire, help you:

- Discern what is from God and what is demonic.
- Interpret the activity you are seeing in the spirit.
- Tap into what God is doing in and through you.
- Manifest breakthroughs for yourself and others.

As you discover the dynamics of this spiritual realm, you will walk in greater knowledge, understanding, and effectiveness in the Kingdom of God.

## Purchase your copy wherever books are sold

From

# Jennifer LeClaire

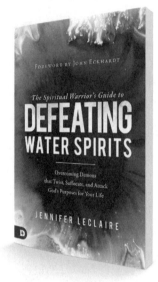

## Gain victory over the spiritual forces of the deep!

What are "water spirits?"

Everyday people are feeling the effects of unseen evil forces, and yet, they don't know what's attacking them, let alone how to have victory.

While many spiritual warriors are familiar with principalities and powers like Jezebel and witchcraft, few have heard of marine demons. Also called "water spirits," these powers wreak havoc in places near bodies of water. From Python, to Leviathan, to Triton to Rahab and beyond, spiritual warriors are feeling the effects of water spirits but often don't know how to combat these evil forces.

Bestselling author Jennifer LeClaire provides a revolutionary guide-book on how to prophetically recognize these spirits and engage in victorious warfare against them. This book will identify each water spirit, equipping believers to overcome them.

Discern the presence of these water spirits and become equipped with spiritual warfare strategies to defeat them!

## Purchase your copy wherever books are sold

From

# Jennifer LeClaire

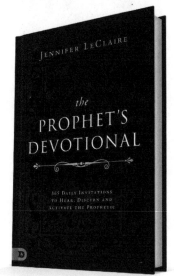

## Daily encouragements to tend the prophetic flame

*The Prophet's Devotional* was written to equip and encourage you in your prophetic gift. No matter where you are in your prophetic journey, this essential resource will sharpen your discernment and hone your delivery of prophetic words.

Bestselling author, spiritual warfare leader, and prophetic trainer, Jennifer LeClaire delivers a devotional experience unlike any other, providing rich, daily teachings and powerful prayers to empower you in your prophetic adventure with the Lord.

As you continue to steward your prophetic gift, you will hear God's voice with greater clarity, and speak His words with greater confidence. What are you waiting for? The adventure begins today!

## Purchase your copy wherever books are sold

# YOUR Prophetic COMMUNITY

Sign up for **FREE** Subscription to the Destiny Image digital magazine, and get awesome content delivered directly to your inbox!

**destinyimage.com/signup**

## Sign-up for Cutting-Edge Messages that Supernaturally Empower You

- Gain valuable insights and guidance based on biblical principles
- Deepen your faith and understanding of God's plan for your life
- Receive regular updates and prophetic messages
- Connect with a community of believers who share your values and beliefs

## Experience Fresh Video Content that Strengthens Your Prophetic Inheritance

- Receive prophetic messages and insights
- Connect with a powerful tool for spiritual growth and development
- Stay connected and inspired on your faith journey

## Listen to Powerful Podcasts that Equips You for God's Presence Everyday

- Deepen your understanding of God's prophetic assignment
- Experience God's revival power throughout your day
- Learn how to grow spiritually in your walk with God

# In the Right Hands, This Book Will Change Lives!

Most of the people who need this message will not be looking for this book. To change their lives, you need to **put a copy of this book in their hands.**

Our ministry is constantly seeking methods to find the people who need this anointed message to change their lives. **Will you help us reach these people?**

**Extend this ministry by sowing 3 books, 5 books, 10 books, or more today, and become a life changer!** Your generosity will be part of catalyzing the Great Awakening that many have been prophesying and praying for.